POCKET GUIDE TO
SELF
HYPNOSIS

ADAM BURKE, Ph.D.

BOOK FAITH INDIA
Delhi

POCKET GUIDE TO SELF HYPNOSIS

Published by
BOOK FAITH INDIA
414-416 Express Tower
Azadpur Commercial Complex
Delhi, India 110033
Tel. [91-11] 713-2459. Fax [91-11] 724-9674
E-mail: pilgrim@del2.vsnl.net.in

Distributed by
PILGRIMS BOOK HOUSE
P.O. Box 3872
Kathmandu, Nepal
Tel. [977-1] 424942. Fax [977-1] 424943.
E-mail: pilgrims@wlink.com.np
WebSite: www.pilgrimsbooks.com

Varanasi Branch
PILGRIMS BOOK HOUSE
B 27/98-A-8, Durga Kund
Varanasi, India 221001
Tel. [91-542] 314060. Fax [91-542] 314059, 312788
E-mail: pilgrim@lw1.vsnl.net.in

Copyright © 1997 by Adam Burke
Cover Illustration and design by Tara M. Eoff

First Book Faith India Edition, 2000
Originally published by The Crossing Press, Inc. in 1997
Printed with permission from the publisher

ISBN 81-7303-226-2

Printed in India

Contents

APPLICATIONS

Preface

Self-hypnosis and imagery are powerful tools. They work by activating a very creative quality of mind. Once activated this deep mind can provide us with the necessary knowledge and power we need to succeed in our lives. With these tools we can begin to build self-loving, confident, highly empowered beliefs. When awakened, the energy of that incredible inner force can be used to improve concentration and learning, enhance sports performance, speed healing, develop deeper friendships, increase our income, and so much, much more.

The process of self-hypnosis is simple, it does not take much time, and the results can be truly incredible. All that is needed is a quiet place to sit, a few minutes to practice, and some basic techniques. For individuals eager to explore this essential life tool, The *Pocket Guide to Self-Hypnosis* is offered as a powerful learning resource. This book presents a palette of techniques for use with a wide variety of issues responsive to hypnotic methods. By following the methods provided, you can begin to make progress on your own goals and feel more in control of your life and your destiny. Working with these tools can empower anyone to move toward his or her dreams with confidence and enthusiasm. The only limit is how big we can dream.

Overview

Chapter One:
How This Book
Can Help You

HYPNOSIS AND FULL POTENTIAL

We all possess far more mental potential than we normally use. Yet much of our potential is not conscious. Another mind, a vast creative inner power, operates beneath our normal conscious awareness. The challenge, if we want to use our full mental potential, is to learn how to open the door to that vast inner world. If we can learn how to use both the surface and the depth of our mind productively, then we open up entirely new possibilities. The key is knowing how to access that deep inner space. Fortunately, access in simple. It just takes some basic knowledge and a few simple techniques that are common to hypnosis.

WHAT IS SELF-HYPNOSIS?

Self-hypnosis is a natural body and mind practice. It uses specific techniques to access a powerful learning state of consciousness. Once inside this creative state we apply positive mental messages and imagery to guide an inner learning process. The outcome, or purpose, of this practice is to generate new actions, feelings, and knowledge for insight, empowerment, healing and increasingly greater life success.

Hypnosis works at the level of our beliefs about ourselves and our world. Family, culture, education, the media, and a myriad of other forces teach many limiting beliefs.

People unwittingly become imprisoned within those rigid mental containers. What keeps those containing forces alive is our learned acceptance that the limits are real. Fortunately, they are often very modifiable if we have a way to unlearn them. With self-hypnosis we can intentionally begin to influence our own beliefs about who we are, why we are here, and what we need to do to be happy. There is really no limit to what we can experience inside, in the creative inner mind. When we learn to work in that space we have a key to open the locks of the old limiting beliefs and free ourselves forever. Once free we can begin to create new beliefs and build new possibilities.

USING MENTAL POWER

Hypnosis uses the mind's capacity to create new realities. An interesting and well documented example of this mental capacity comes from the placebo literature. In this research many hundreds of studies have shown how peoples' beliefs affect their emotions, behaviors, and even their physiology.

The term placebo comes from the Latin. The translation is, "I will please." Placebo treatments, from the classic sugar pill to the injections of saline solution, have shown positive effects with high blood pressure, headaches, depression, ulcers, hay fever, arthritis, pain and more. They have the potential to influence almost any condition. Obviously what we believe to be true is very powerful medicine. Self-hypnosis fundamentally builds new positive beliefs for greater growth and success.

DREAMS AND THE HYPNOTIC EXPERIENCE

One way to understand the hypnotic experience is to compare it to the dream process. In our dreams we experience images and feelings as real, although they are obviously just dreams. Because they seem real we react to them as we would react to waking state experiences. If we are being chased by a tiger in our dream, we might awaken frightened, with our heart racing. Similarly, hypnosis works with ideas and images in a deeper, creative state of mind. In this state the images take on a reality of their own. We can explore new possibilities about ourselves as if they are real. We can experience earning more money, skiing a perfect slalom, being healed and healthy, whatever we want. Because the mind is experiencing these things as if they are real, we begin to discover new ways of being.

Another similarity to dreams is the flexibility of the trance mind. The trance mind is not limited by logic. You can fly your bicycle to an English garden to have a conversation with a long-departed loved one. In the dream it all seems quite plausible and natural. In the hypnotic trance state the mind can consider all types of possibilities that would not be believable to the conscious mind because of learned limits. In this state, the normal controlling filters of the conscious mind are temporarily reduced, so we can experience previously unbelievable visions of our potential. In this way self-hypnosis can be very powerful in helping us to modify limiting beliefs at their root.

By contrast, there is a major difference between dreams and hypnosis. Dreams are basically random events for most people, not planned or intentional. The hypnotic experience is directed by our intention to change or improve specific aspects of our life. In self-hypnosis we *direct* the focus of our inner work. Self-hypnosis specifically channels the energy of the deep mind to help us find answers to very specific questions. Also, hypnosis is not sleep. In a hypnotic trance, as compared to sleep, the body is generally more relaxed and the brain waves more active than in sleep.

A NATURAL STATE

Trance is a natural state. We go in and out of altered states all the time. We daydream. We go for a drive with a friend, have a deep conversation, and arrive at our destination before we know it, amazed at how fast the time went by. We read a book or watch a movie and become completely engrossed. We overhear a conversation about grandparents and our mind spins off into a vivid memory of our grandparents. During such moments the mind does not go away—it just shifts to a more internal place that is less distracted. That is the mind we use in self-hypnosis. An ability to focus and temporarily reduce the normal sensory input is part of our nature. We use that process all day long. It just comes and goes without our intention. Our minds can go into that inner place while driving a car, watching a movie, or reading a book. It is possible to do it any time or place. It is part of the way we know the world.

PHYSIOLOGY OF TRANCE

Hypnosis is a natural body and mind phenomenon. In addition to shifts in perception, hypnosis produces a constellation of physiological changes. Early researchers in the

1930s expected the EEG patterns for hypnosis to resemble those of deep sleep—predominantly delta and theta frequencies. Logically so, as the term hypnosis was derived from the Greek word *hypnos*, to sleep. Research has consistently shown, however, that during hypnosis we generally find an increase in the production of alpha rhythms compared to the slow delta and theta activity of deep sleep. This EEG pattern in hypnosis is similar to that of relaxation. In addition, we find an increase in basal skin resistance (BSR) (there is an inverse relationship between BSR and arousal), decreases in respiration, metabolism, and cardiac output, and an increase in body temperature. So essentially, hypnosis looks similar to relaxation physiologically, while cognitively we could say it looks more like dreaming. The physiological relaxation reduces resistance to change, helping the hypnotic suggestion to produce insight and new ways of being.

DEPTH OF TRANCE

People often have a belief that hypnotic trance is a state of oblivion, of being unaware of everything that is going on. That is probably where people's fear of loss of control comes from when they think of hypnosis. In reality, however, there are many levels of trance individuals experience in hypnosis, from light to deep. In a very deep trance the individual will not be aware of the external environment, as the mental focus will be very internal. In a lighter trance, however, the environment remains in the awareness. The important thing to remember is that the goal of hypnosis is not the subjective experience, but rather the outcome of the trancework. My experience over the years has shown me that people can have shallow and deep trances and both trance states get very positive results. The results are what matters, and I have not found deeper subjective trance states to necessarily produce any better results.

KNOW WHEN TO USE OTHER FORMS OF HELP

Everything has a time and a place. You would not paint a house with a hammer. You could do it, but it would be very slow and inefficient. Self-hypnosis is not a replacement for professional treatment. Someone with a serious problem, whether it is physical, emotional, social or spiritual, will benefit from professional attention. You cannot see your own face without a mirror to reflect it back. A potential limitation of self-treatment involves not seeing the actual problem or the best solution. We are often the last to really understand our own issues, in part due to the self-protective nature of the habitual mind. Also, symptoms can be misleading. I had a friend, for example, with persistent headaches. Both she and her doctor thought she had sinus problems. When her doctor was away on holiday, she saw his office partner. He became suspicious of the symptoms and sent her for scans. She had a very serious brain tumor. That was a year after the headaches started. The point is that we need self-care *and* professional care. There is a time and place for both. Working with a skillful professional can often help remedy the problem faster and more completely. If professional care does indeed turn out to be the best strategy, then self-hypnosis can be a great adjunct treatment. Be open to receiving the help you need from others, be it doctor, clergy, or coach, in addition to healing yourself.

CONCLUDING THOUGHT

Hypnosis is a powerful medicine. It cannot do the impossible, but it can do amazing things if used wisely. I sense that in the West we are just scratching the surface regarding what is possible with this incredible tool. We are standing at the edge of time and space looking out into a vast field of possibilities. Now it is your time to learn this knowledge. When you have completed reading this book, you will have a good sense of what hypnosis is and what it is capable of. You will have a variety of methods for working on your own issues deeply and effectively. You can even use these ideas to develop self-guiding audio tapes for your own success. Everything you need to begin is in here, and with patience and practice you will find it to be a profoundly important personal tool. Good luck and have fun.

Chapter Two:
Understanding Hypnosis and Trance

Over the years I have taught countless individuals how to do self-hypnosis. I like to teach it to people because it is easy to learn and because it can be so powerful. Given the reports from clients and students, and the changes I see in their lives, I know it works. So let us look deeper into what hypnosis is, and there is no better way to do that than to begin practicing self-hypnosis right now.

A ONE MINUTE METHOD

If you are like me, you do not want to read an entire book to find out how to do something. You want to get going now. This book is full of principles, techniques, and applications that will help you to become quite skillful at working with trance over time. For those of you eager to begin now, however, the essence of all of those skills can be condensed into this simple formula:

- Induce and deepen a quietly focused body and mind learning state.
- Send transformative ideas/suggestions to that deep body and mind state.

So, for those of you in a hurry, here is a One Minute Method to try right now.

- Sit or lie comfortably.
- Close your eyes.

- Take three deep breaths and release all tension.
- Do this:
  — Imagine you are holding a two-inch energy ball in your hand.
  — Squeeze it—physically squeeze it.
  — Pretend that the harder you squeeze the more it resists, and that your forces match equally; you cannot modify the shape of the ball.
  — Tell yourself, "The harder I squeeze the deeper I go inside."
  — Continue to squeeze for a minute; then absolutely, totally, completely release everything.
- Feel yourself dropping down deep inside.
- Give yourself your suggestion, "I am very healthy, or productive, or happy, etc."
  — See the desired outcome; see a future image of that outcome.
  — Feel the positive feelings associated with that outcome.
  — Hear any sounds associated with that outcome.
- Come back feeling refreshed, relaxed, and ready for action.

Ta dah! Now let's look into the origins of hypnosis.

A BRIEF HISTORY

Every culture has its methods of inducing trance. Shamans throughout the world use dancing, drumming, chanting, and other means to self-induce trance to access inner resources for the benefit of their communities. Indeed, throughout time and place, we find humanity tapping into this innate capacity for self-knowledge as a path to personal transformation and social good.

The variation we know of as hypnosis historically began its evolution during the 18th century in western Europe. It was a fertile time in which the interplay of new ideas in science, medicine, and religion germinated powerfully transforming discoveries and understandings. An Austrian physician, Franz Anton Mesmer (1734–1815), is frequently associated with the beginnings of modern hypnosis. Mesmer developed a large following around a method he called animal magnetism. Although Mesmer himself was ultimately rebuked by the scientific community, his ideas and those of his contemporaries took on a fervor of their own. In the 19th century a wave of investigation and debate ensued in medicine and psychology in Europe. James Braid, a Scottish physician, coined the term hypnosis, and Pierre Janet, the French psychologist, popularized the term subconscious. During this highly productive period, the understanding and practice of hypnosis began to earn a credible and substantiated place in therapy and healing.

During the 20th century, hypnosis came to be widely used as a treatment for traumatic stress disorders and other problems in World Wars I and II and the Korean War. Hypnotherapy training and research continues to evolve in the professional community today. Hypnotic methods have also grown in popularity among the general public, with increasing numbers of audio tapes, books, and training programs available on the subject. Although its history is colorful and filled with a struggle for acceptance in the West, its importance cannot be denied or ignored.

MYTHS AND FACTS ABOUT HYPNOSIS

First, therapeutic hypnosis is not stage hypnosis. Stage hypnosis is supposed to be entertainment, so the focus is on getting people to do funny things, not on healing. In reality most of stage hypnosis is not hypnotic trance. It is more typically role-playing by the participants.

A second common misunderstanding is a presumed loss of control. People might fear revealing deep, dark secrets, or doing things against their will. In reality it takes a certain willingness to be hypnotized. All organisms have a self-protective tendency. This does not go away in trance.

Another misperception is that hypnotic subjects are suggestible and that being suggestible is bad. The key thing to remember is that suggestibility is not gullibility. Highly suggestible people are highly suggestible, not highly gullible. There is actually a positive correlation between IQ and hypnotizability—the higher the IQ the more hypnotizable one is.

The final misperception is that hypnosis can help individuals to do things outside of the realistic limits of their potential. Hypnosis can take us to the edge of our potential, but not beyond what is humanly possible for us.

Hypnotic trancework is definitely wild and wonderful stuff. It is something that has been with humanity for as long as history has been recorded and undoubtedly much longer. It uses our basic capacity to go inside, into a vast inner realm of possibilities, to find new ideas and essential answers. The trance world is a great sky above our heads in which we can dream of what life will become.

The Process

Chapter Three:
Preparing for Self-Hypnosis

A little preparation can sometimes make a big difference between success and failure. Everyone has taken exams in school, and everyone knows that studying before an exam generally improves the outcome. Study time prepares you and supports your success. Similarly, before you sit down to do self-hypnosis work, you will want to prepare. This will help to make your sessions maximally effective. The four requisite preparatory elements are: Right Attitude, Right Setting, Right Goal, and Right Method.

RIGHT ATTITUDE

As described in the previous chapter, people often think of hypnosis as mind control or some other negative phenomena. Quite the contrary, hypnosis taps into one of our most creative inner resources, accessing a tremendous capacity for healing and empowerment. Having a positive, informed attitude about your hypnotic practice will make it even more productive. To that end it will be useful to briefly consider the following ideas: expectation, patience and persistence, taking action, gratitude, and being open to learn.

Positive Expectations

Positive expectations will increase your success. Hypnosis is powerful and the more you allow things to happen, and expect things to happen, the better. Your positive expectancy will help support the process. Imagine the following situation. Two seven-year-olds are playing their first piano recitals. One child has a supportive parent who always encourages her to do her best. The other child has a parent who always expects her to fail. Which child will perform better at that recital and enjoy the process more? Life is more pleasant and productive when our loved ones support our success. The same can be said for encouraging and believing in ourselves too. Be your own pep squad. Expect the best from your self-hypnotic practice.

Patience and Persistence

Change is a process. People who want everything to be better or different overnight, without any commitment or doing on their part, are going to be frustrated souls. A very wealthy businessman once said that a person needs to know two things to make money. The first is knowing what you want. The second is determining if you will be willing to do what it takes to get it. Successful self-hypnotic transformation requires two qualities—patience and persistence. One of the simple reasons that many people do not succeed in life is because they lack persistence. They give up too early. The sad thing is that they may be well on their way and then they give up, like the guy in the joke who swam halfway to Hawaii, then turned around because it was too far. Hypnosis is very powerful, but it will not change our lives overnight. Most things take time. If you hang in there with your dream, and use trancework to catalyze it, that dream will come faster.

Taking Action

Self-hypnosis is not a magical process. If your hypnotic suggestions are for a larger income, it will probably not happen because the sweepstakes patrol comes to your door. It is more likely that those suggestions will stimulate your inner mind to give you clues about who to talk to, which want ads to look at, knowing if you need to move to a new city, having the courage to follow your dreams, feeling more confidence in your skills, and having greater clarity about what your unique gift is. Often hypnosis changes lives by empowering people to take action, moving them toward their dreams more confidently.

Gratitude

It might sound funny that gratitude could improve success, but it can. Gratitude is essentially a state of appreciation for what we have. If we practice gratitude for the little changes as they happen, we build enthusiasm for our growing success. If we refuse to be satisfied until we have the mansion, then our negative mind state may slow our progress. The answers may look different than we expect them to. If we are not grateful for the little changes, we may completely miss the fact that the answer is coming through now, because we are looking for something else. Gratitude in its own right is a very powerful healing attitude. If we all had more gratitude for life's simple pleasures, the world would be a much better place.

Being Open to Learn

Self-hypnosis activates a powerful part of our nature. It is important to have a respectful relationship with that place.

If we work with it wisely, it will be a valuable resource in our life. When we do our practice, the results will come at the perfect time and in the perfect way. There is an inner wisdom at work here, so the answers may look different than what we expect or want. We have to be open to learn from this deep place. It can be humbling. Hypnosis elicits a large help system. Appreciate and honor that inner wisdom. Used wisely, it will amaze you.

RIGHT SETTING

One of the nice things about hypnosis is that it requires no special circumstances, no special garb or postures, no special context. You can do it almost anywhere and any time. Once you have the skill, you can drop into your hypnotic work space in short order. It becomes quite easy to mix it into the events of the day as needed.

Ideal Conditions

It is possible to do self-hypnosis almost anywhere since you are working inside of a mind-space, a virtual environment if you will. Yet despite this flexibility, it is desirable to have an appropriate setting. Ideally you will want to use a quiet and calm location. Music is always helpful as it creates a secondary source of distraction, absorption or emotional evocation. Well chosen music can help elicit particular states of emotion useful for channeling the work in different directions. As a general rule, select quieting and relaxing music, as calmness facilitates trance. Turning down the lights will help reduce sensory input. Put pets outside of the room. They will be attracted to your quietness and will want to sit on your lap, which will be distracting. If you have children or a partner tell them you need a few minutes of quiet time and close the door. Do not do hypnosis right after a meal, if possible, as the blood is shunted to digestion and alertness decreases. You may fall asleep at that time and trance is not sleep. Similarly, doing it late at night can also be challenging as the relaxation of trance may put you to sleep.

Less Ideal Conditions

If you find yourself doing your hypnotic practice at the office, on the road, or in the million other less-than-perfect places of life, try to find a quiet corner, out of the way if possible. Close your eyes and do your inner work. Hypnosis can be completely invisible. No one will know what you are doing. It will look like you are resting for a few minutes, when in reality you have an entire change process occurring within. Whenever I fly, I often do several hours of inner work. To those around me it looks like I am asleep. This is very helpful if you do not feel like talking to anyone. Because self-hypnosis is not very context sensitive, you can do it when you need it, wherever you are. When I find my mental wheels spinning and I am accomplishing little, I take a five minute self-hypnosis break to focus my mind and get back on track. That usually does the trick.

RIGHT GOAL

Probably one of the greatest benefits of doing self-hypnotic work regularly is that it makes you begin to think about what you really want in life. Doing self-hypnosis regularly starts to focus your mind on what you dream of having, being and doing. That alone is an extremely powerful benefit. It is a statement to your unconscious mind that your dreams matter, that you deserve to be happy, that you believe there is a way to move towards those dreams, and that you are now taking responsibility for making your life work the way you want it to.

Clarify Your Goals

You can do hypnosis for relaxation and pleasant feelings, and that is great. Typically, however, people do it because they have some issue or goal they want to make progress on. They want to modify or improve some behavior, condition, belief or habit. The clearer we can be about that goal, that desired outcome, the better. This is important because we use that goal to build our hypnotic suggestions. If our goal is clear, our hypnotic suggestions will be more direct and powerful, and it is the suggestion that generates new patterns. This goal clarification process can take some time, but it is time well spent. You would not ask Santa Claus for a car, as he might bring you a junker. You would ask for a specific color, model, style, and year. Be as clear and specific as possible. Thinking about your destination, your goal, is very important. If you are unclear regarding the best goal, then you can use hypnosis to get clear. First use self-hypnosis to clarify your goal. Then use it to achieve that goal. Always try to start with a sense of where you want to go.

Know Your Values

For a goal to be truly powerful it has to be built upon the foundation of your life values. If goals do not have a value foundation, then they may actually be counterproductive. For example, if you have a goal that in reality runs against a deeper personal value, then you will probably encounter unconscious resistance to progress on that goal. Part of you is obstructing your progress because the goal cuts against your deeper personal sense of meaning. For example, a used car lot is having a contest for its sales staff. The person who sells the most cars gets a free trip to Hawaii. A new sales-woman thinks it will be fun to go to Hawaii, so she decides to sell as many cars as she can. The easiest way to do that would be to lie about the quality of the cars. This woman, however, strongly values the importance of honesty. In this case her honesty value will probably make it hard for her to make easy money through dishonest sales. Her deeper value will obstruct a more superficial goal. To the extent that our goals match our values, there will be more passion and ener-gy behind them. Look at what a goal will bring you. Explore its highest benefit. Then see if it matches your personally motivating values. If it does, it will have power.

Determining the Issue

In addition to values and goals, it is helpful to know what the problem, challenge, or issue is. This requires some thoughtful diagnosis. Why diagnose the problem at all? Because if we do not know what is broken, we will not know what to fix. When mechanics work on cars, they do an ini-tial diagnosis to determine whether the problem is electri-cal, mechanical, or just being out of fuel. Without that step their work will be less efficient.

In diagnosing a human issue it is helpful to think of life as a sphere. This sphere has three levels. At the center of the sphere is the person. The middle sphere is behavior. The outer sphere is the environment. So the sphere consists of three dynamically interacting elements: the person, their behaviors, and the environment with which the person interacts.

The person includes everything that happens inside of the skin—thoughts, feelings, internal body states or physiology, sensory processes, ego experience (the sense of I), and spirit. Behavior can include compulsive actions, addictive habits, interpersonal challenges, positive actions, deepening talents, new skills being perfected, many things. Behaviors are active and passive, verbal and nonverbal. The environment includes social, physical, and biological factors. These elements also interact through time. We have a past, present and future, all of which affect our life at every moment to some degree.

Person

I have worked with more than a few people on weight management issues. One woman I helped had spent much of her adult life going from one diet to another. Like so many people, she attributed her weight issue to eating the wrong foods, in the wrong amounts, at the wrong time. All of her solutions, however, were temporary. Like most dieters, she would chronically gain the weight back despite her best efforts. After our conversations it became apparent she was eating to appease emotional needs—feelings of pain, sadness, and loss. We did some hypnotic work at that level and also included the important specific suggestions of eating healthy, lower calorie foods and exercising. During the ensuing months, without much effort, she lost about thirty pounds. More importantly, she has become a happier, more integrated person. The weight issue has become less of a focus as her life is coming into a more natural balance.

Behavior

A former client had been seeing a psychologist for many months. The psychologist had been analyzing her relationship with her father as a possible cause of her high anxiety. She came to my acupuncture office for another issue and happened to mention the anxiety. In my interview I asked her if she drank coffee. Well did she ever, literally over a gallon a day of caffeinated coffee. So what do you think I did? You guessed. I suggested she cut down to eight cups a day. The next week she came in and told me that she was feeling much less anxiety. What a surprise. So here she was being treated for anxiety with the assumption it was psychological. I was amazed that her therapist had never asked her about coffee, but therapists are mind people, not body people. We always see the world through the filter of our professional training. Her problem was not an emotional one, it was a coffee drinking habit—a behavior. We got her to cut down on coffee, change a behavior, and her anxiety improved dramatically. She stopped therapy.

Environment

I once had a client with chronic back pain. He was receiving medical attention to no avail. He came for hypnosis. It was revealed that the symptoms only appeared when he was having difficulties in his marriage. My assessment was that this was his unconscious mind's way of telling him to heal his home life. He had been in a lot of denial about his marital difficulties, wanting to have a happy family. His body, however, was trying to tell him to pay attention to this issue, a social environment issue, before it got worse. We reframed the issue, did some work on healthy relationships, and got the couple into counseling. Their relationship and his problem both improved. Interestingly, the only time it acts up is when they are off balance, which provides him useful information he can use to stay more conscious about the healthiness of his social environment. That is body brilliance.

Time

The interplay of person, behavior and environment all happen through time. We have a past, present and future. Self-hypnosis is generally not as focused on the past as some therapies are. It is more solution-oriented, focused on the present and future. It emphasizes where we are now and where we want to be. That is one of the things I love so much about this method. You do not have to know why you have your challenges. You only have to be aware of where you want to end up, what kind of life you want to have. There are certain types of hypnosis that deal more with the past, such as traumatic incidents of childhood. If that is what you really want or need, that is beyond the scope of this book. You would be best served doing that type of hypnotic work with a licensed therapist who does hypnosis. It is important to have someone qualified to guide that process in the event the material that surfaces is disturbing to you.

Not Knowing Is Fine

The counterpoint to all of this is that it can be very difficult at times to ascertain the actual cause of our issues. The causal path can be complex, having evolved over years of abuse or neglect. Typically there is not a single thing we can point our finger at and say "That's it." The wonderful thing about the trance mind is that, like water, it will find the deepest roots if it is allowed to move. If we ask for healing, it will search out that root level even if we do not know consciously what or where that might be. With hypnosis the healing can occur without our even knowing what the cause is. The issue will just be healed. This inner wisdom mind is an intelligent search and repair mechanism. We simply have to put it into motion and it will proceed to do the work. If we focus on the solution, the hypnotic mind will help us find the path to that goal. As long as we have a sense of what we want, and we ask our inner mind for help in getting it, that mind will move us toward our goal.

RIGHT METHOD

Before we proceed to the specific techniques of self-hypnosis, it would be helpful to get a quick overview of the five step model we will be learning. Each of the elements of this process will be explained in detail in the upcoming chapters.

Select goals/objectives and prepare for session (Chapter 3).
As described in this chapter, it is important to prepare for your hypnotic session. Determine what the issue is. If possible direct the work to the appropriate level of the issue—person, behavior, or environment. Also, determine what it is that you want, your desired goal or outcome.

Induce a trance state (Chapter 4).
Induction methods take the mind from the external to the internal, from the diffuse to the focused. These methods withdraw the attention from the outer world, helping to quiet the mind and the body. In Chapter 4 we will examine a number of powerful induction methods for going into trance quickly and easily.

Deepen the trance (Chapter 5).

Once the trance mind is engaged you will want to deepen that state. If we were to describe the induction process as entering a house, then deepening would be like proceeding into the house to explore other rooms. There are many methods for deepening that we will examine in Chapter 5, including guided imagery, hypnotic phenomena, and direct suggestion.

Give self-hypnotic suggestions (Chapter 6).

With the deep mind activated we are more responsive to suggestions. Hypnotic suggestion is a fundamental element in our trancework. These suggestions are like the rain that washes away the old residue and creates new pathways. We will examine hypnotic suggestions in Chapter 6.

Conclude trance and return to a conscious state of mind (Chapter 7).

At this point the trancework has been done; the suggestions have been given. Now it is time to come back from the trance, ready for action. This step offers an opportunity to provide final suggestions, to facilitate future trancework, to deepen the effect of the current session, and to come back prepared for a great day. This will be explained fully in Chapter 7.

Length of Sessions

One of the nicest things about hypnosis is that it does not take much time. All you really need is a few minutes, literally, to do some work. I call self-hypnosis Guerrilla Therapy because it is a quick, anytime, anywhere process. You can easily do a number of brief sessions throughout the day as needed. You can do micro-sessions right before an event, such as a sport performance or an exam. Actually, short sessions during the day are probably better for self-hypnosis than one long session, since it may be harder to find the time to do long sessions. Just a few minutes of practice now and then will begin to set a new pattern in motion. Of course if you do have the time, you can do a twenty minute session or even longer, but mini-sessions work great.

Chapter Four:
Induction Methods

The hypnotic state we utilize for this transformational work is different than normal waking consciousness. Giving yourself suggestions in hypnosis is not like giving yourself a suggestion in normal waking consciousness. In hypnosis we give suggestions to a deeper, inner mind, which then works with those ideas to construct new possibilities. For hypnosis to do its work we need to access or induce that deep inner mind.

The induction methods we are about to examine provide an entry point to the deep trance mind. Induction methods are specific techniques that take us from outside to inside, from conscious mind to inner mind. The induction process is like entering a friend's house and standing in the entryway. We have entered the house, no longer outside, but we have not yet begun to move deeply into the structure to examine the various work spaces. The induction is that transitional zone we migrate through when moving from conscious mind to deep mind.

INDUCTION METHODS

Induction methods are focusing techniques. They help the mind to transition from the active outer consciousness to a quieter, more internal state. Depending on the method employed, that transition can occur gradually or very abruptly. There are many different types of induction methods. All of them essentially disengage the conscious linear mind, temporarily slowing down the normal thought processes and focusing mental awareness. This puts the body and mind in better position to receive suggestions for inner work.

Have you ever noticed that a loud, sudden noise can cause the breath to momentarily stop, the mind to quiet, and the awareness to orient toward the sound? The state may only last for a moment while the sound is being analyzed, but in that moment the body and mind are still and focused. That shift from normal mind to quiet focus is an induction into a new state, a state ready for responding and learning. Induction methods employ a variety of strategies to elicit that centering effect. So let us examine the different approaches to induction. Experiment with them and find an induction method that feels best to you.

Inner Focus

Inner focus, as the name implies, is the process of directing the attention inward, as in meditation. In ancient India, preparatory techniques called Pratyahara were practiced prior to meditation. Pratyahara methods were used to withdraw the mind from the sense channels, taking the focus inside. To a large extent that is what the hypnotic induction methods do. When the mind begins to focus on the inner condition, such as breathing, body position, or muscular relaxation, there is a movement away from the distractions of the outer world toward a more narrowly focused inner awareness. This focusing helps prepare the body and mind for trance.

Practice: Lie down comfortably and scan through your body, slowly noticing how it feels. Tell yourself mentally that you are lying down, that you feel your legs, your arms, your head on the cushion. Describe in some detail what you feel, such as pulsing, twitches, vibration, warmth. Focus on pleasant rather than unpleasant sensations. This method serves to focus the mind on the moment. It is similar to the Buddhist mindfulness meditation practice known as Vipassana. Practicing this body scan and feedback process can be very centering. You will probably find it to be a very relaxing practice.

Repetitive Patterns

Have you ever been mesmerized listening to the sound of ocean waves or a gentle spring rain? Perhaps nine months in the womb listening to the muffled sound of a beating heart trains the mind to find comfort in rhythm. Not surprisingly, numerous induction methods employ the repetition of monotonous, rhythmical, sensory stimuli for fixing attention. An example of this is the visual repetition of a swinging watch or pendulum.

Practice: Anything with a repetitive visual pattern in your environment, such as a moving clock pendulum, can be used as an induction vehicle. Auditory methods are also useful. One pleasant and very effective method is to use some type of music that you enjoy. There is quite a bit of ambient music around these days—new age or space music—that is perfect for this type of work. It is not totally monotonic, but it does have a soothing rhythmical nature. Get music that is relaxing and slowing. Some of the environmental sound pieces work very well in this regard, such as the sounds of ocean waves or rain, as they provide the natural auditory rhythms we love. Allow yourself to watch or hear the pattern and notice how your body and mind feel as they become entrained with the rhythm.

Mental Fixation

In this approach we focus on some object to center our attention. Just like a honeybee enamored with the flower and its nectar, as the mind is engaged in something attractive, the normal stream of thought begins to slow down, creating the potential for entering trance.

Practice: One method that people find very pleasant involves attending to certain body spaces, such as the space between the two eyebrows, or at the heart region. Just feel the energy there. It is subtle but present. The area between the two eyebrows, for example, can be experienced as tingling energy or a ball of warm light. One of the ancient Indian Pratyahara methods is a technique called tratak. In tratak you gaze steadily at some object, such as a candle flame. The reduced optic input, if one can actually keep the gaze relatively still, has the effect of quieting the mind. You can also use a painting on the wall, or a tree, or any other pleasant stimuli to gaze at. All of these methods gently hold the mind's attention, allowing it to become quiet and restful.

Creative Imaging

This method uses the mind's ability to generate absorbing images. It is like daydreaming. When the mind is engaged in a daydream we lose track of the world around us and become open to new ideas and inner experiences.

Practice: Think of a place you have actually been to that is particularly comforting, relaxing, and safe, such as a mountain meadow or the ocean. As you begin to remember that scene, you will automatically be drawn inside. You can also use your favorite science fiction or fantasy environments, as long as they are safe, relaxing scenes. A last method is to find a place of comfort or safety or joy inside. Imagine what color, shape, temperature and sound it would possess. Let yourself go into that place.

Hypnotic Phenomena

This method employs powerful hypnotic tools called Hypnotic Phenomena. These will be explained in more detail in Chapter 5. For the moment, however, we can say that they are both ways into trance and effects of trance.

Practice: Catalepsy (paralysis) is one of the more common hypnotic phenomena used for induction. Catalepsy means that a body part is locked or temporarily immovable, such as the hands being stuck together. For this practice, bring your hands together and interlace the fingers. Press your hands together, telling yourself that they are becoming locked— they are melting together. If you are good at this particular phenomenon, you will not be able to pull them apart until you tell yourself you can.

Direct Suggestion

Finally, you can enter the trance state by telling your mind that you are going inside. This is a helpful practice to use with any of the induction methods you choose. Whichever one you employ, it is generally useful to tell yourself that you are going deeper and deeper inside, moving towards a very powerful, wise, and creative part of yourself.

Practice: Sit quietly with the eyes closed. Notice how your body feels. Tell yourself mentally that you feel wonderful, that your body feels very relaxed, quiet, calm and wonderful. Do this again for several minutes, then notice how your body feels. Typically, it will be more relaxed and quiet. Now tell yourself that you are going deeper into relaxation and peace. Repeat this for a few minutes. Stop and notice the feelings. Direct suggestion can be very productive. Often all we need is to give ourselves some inner direction, some inner leadership. This method awakens your inner self-leader.

Am I in Trance Yet?

There are a variety of hypnotic symptoms or indicators that let you know you are entering an altered state. These can be mild or strong, and they will vary from session to session. They are just things to notice, not essentials. They can include: small twitching movements as the muscles respond to inner images and relaxation; reduced heart rate and breathing; increased muscular relaxation; slower responses and movements; increased circulation in the periphery, stomach sounds as the body begins to relax and digestion increases; and increased responsiveness to suggestion.

OTHER HELPFUL IDEAS

Accept the Experiences as They Come

An accepting state of mind is very helpful. Allow everything that is experienced to be perfect just the way it is. There are going to be noises in the environment, carpenters hammering, buses going by. If you make those noises bad, thinking they are an annoyance, then they will indeed be an annoyance. The best thing to do is to incorporate them into the experience by telling the mind that these sounds will help you go deeper. Use the same approach for any potentially distracting signal. Tell your mind that everything you feel, hear, think or imagine, on any level, is just going to help you to go deeper into a wonderful state of relaxation and peace. There are no distractions. Everything will help you to go deeper.

Use the pleasant experiences too. Perhaps you are doing your practice outside and you feel the warmth of the sun on your skin. You may have some beautiful, relaxing music playing, or you can smell the flowers on the table. Allow these pleasant things to open your gratitude. The grateful mind is very quiet and focused because it is content.

Trust Your Process

The trance experience will often vary from session to session. Some sessions will be faster and deeper than others. You can imagine how frustration with that variability could be counterproductive to a state of inner focus and peace. You cannot have both inner peace and frustration—they are contradictory states. Trust your process. One of the wonderful ironies of hypnosis is that you cannot try harder to do better. The harder you try the less you get. It is in letting go that the state occurs. When I work with clients, I sometimes have to tell the overachieving individuals to let it happen. Their trying to help gets in the way of their outcome. Perhaps it is a good lesson for our Western minds that, at least with hypnosis, doing requires being. Go with the Force.

EFFECTIVE INDUCTION METHODS

Here are a few specific induction methods to try now. Experiment with them and see which work best for you.

Eyes—Up/Closed/Down

This is a simple and effective method that I often teach clients for their self-hypnosis practice. There are three steps to the process. You can do it sitting or lying down. Look straight ahead with a relaxed gaze at something peaceful, such as a blank wall or out the window at a tree or the sky. Still looking straight ahead, inhale. Keep your head still and as you inhale, raise your gaze up. When you have finished your inhale, hold your breath and close your eyelids. Hold the breath for the count of ten. During this count your eyes are still looking up with the eyelids closed. When you reach ten, exhale quickly, letting the eyes lower. As you do this, totally release your muscles and allow yourself to experience a sense that your body is dropping. The sensation is like gently falling through your chair. It is very pleasant. You can repeat this process two or three times. Each time open your eyes a bit less with the inhale. Inhale, look up without moving the head, close the eyelids and hold the breath. Count to ten mentally. Exhale, lowering the eyes. Feel the body dropping down and relax into that feeling.

The Sinking Pearl

Another method is to sit comfortably and feel yourself sinking down, as if you are a pearl or a stone. Feel yourself just sinking down through warm blue water. You feel the warm water flowing by you as you sink deeper into that wonderful feeling. Imagine yourself eventually coming to rest on a soft sandy bottom. The warm currents move you ever so slightly until you find the perfect resting point, a place of complete ease. You rest there and enjoy that feeling of deep comfort. Feel the vibration of comfort in your entire body.

Locked Eyelids

One of the more common catalepsy techniques is the locked eyelids. In this method you sit comfortably and gaze at some object, such as a picture, or blank wall. Tell yourself that the eyelids are getting very heavy, very heavy. Keep gazing and telling yourself that your eyelids are very heavy, they want to close. Soon your eyelids will feel heavy and will close. Next, you begin to suggest the catalepsy. You repeat to yourself that your eyelids are so heavy that they will not be able to open. Use phrases like, "My eyelids are so incredibly and wonderfully heavy." Words like "wonderful" and "comfortable" allow the mind to understand that it is a positive heaviness. This increases the incentive for the eyes to close. Tell yourself that as the eyes close and become fixed together, you will go deeper and deeper inside, into a wonderful place of healing and creativity. Keep repeating the phrase, allowing your eyes to become heavier and heavier until they close shut. Tell yourself they are incredibly heavy, locked shut, wonderfully, comfortably heavy, so heavy you could not open them even if you wanted to. Try to open them, try hard if you want. Tell yourself the more you try to open them the more locked they become, taking you deeper and deeper inside. You can test the lock if you want. If you are good at this method, your eyelids will not open until you allow them to. Be aware of your locked eyelids and allow yourself to flow deeper. When you are ready to come out, tell yourself that your eyelids are releasing and that they feel perfect. Then come out of the trance.

Chapter Five:
Relaxation and Deepening

In the previous chapter the induction process was compared to coming into the house and stepping into the entryway. Continuing that analogy, the deepening component of self-hypnosis is like proceeding into the house toward the work areas. First we enter trance (induction), then we deepen the state for greater creative potential (deepening). In this chapter we will examine a variety of effective methods for that deepening process. Special consideration will be given to relaxation as a deepening method because of the unique therapeutic value it provides. Other deepening techniques we will explore include counting down, imagery, and hypnotic phenomena.

RELAXATION

People typically find hypnosis very relaxing, which is one of the reasons they enjoy doing it. Although relaxation is not necessary for deep trance to occur, it is a very common and useful element. One reason we focus on relaxation as a basic part of our session is that it is therapeutic in its own right. Relaxation therapy has been found to help muscular tension, headaches, neck and back pain, high blood pressure, mild phobias, insomnia and depression. It is safe, effective, and easy to learn. Although relaxation alone is therapeutic, it is even more productive as part of hypnosis. This is because the addition of imagery and hypnotic suggestion significantly increases the specific focus of the work and consequently produces much more powerful effects.

Relaxation Practices

Several self-hypnosis relaxation techniques will now be described. Try them and find the one that feels the best to you. Then employ it as part of your self-hypnosis process. When you do these exercises, you will want to do them in a comfortable position. Obviously comfort facilitates relaxation. To maximize your relaxation experience, lie down on a couch or the floor, or sit in a large chair in which your head is supported and your feet and legs are comfortable. Take off glasses and shoes. Loosen any restrictive articles, such as ties, belts, and watches. Have a blanket to cover you if necessary (you will want to stay warm enough). Turn on some pleasant, relaxing music.

Direct Suggestion

One of the simplest methods for relaxation is direct suggestion. The body responds to requests we give it. If we tell ourselves enough times that we feel energetic or tired, then we will move in that direction (within certain limits of course). You may remember the research on placebos described in Chapter 2 that showed how profoundly the mind can affect the body.

To help create physical relaxation, make direct suggestions that your body is relaxed. The key words that work well for most people are "warm, heavy, and relaxed." Repeat those words over and over: "My body feels warm, heavy, and relaxed." It is useful to focus that suggestion initially to specific body parts, especially the large muscle masses of the arms and legs. Tell your arms that they are feeling warm, heavy and relaxed. Then tell your legs that they are feeling warm, heavy, and relaxed. Focus on an area. Repeat the phrase several times. Then notice the feelings in that area for five to ten seconds. Those feelings may include tingling, warmth, muscular relaxation, and other pleasant sensations. Initially, direct the suggestions to parts of the body where they will be believable. If you tend to have cold hands and feet you may want to attend to those areas later, after first relaxing the arms and legs. In the initial phase focus on the larger muscle groups, such as the legs and arms.

Counting Down

A common method for deepening relaxation is counting. You may have seen a television program in which a hypnotist was counting backwards from one hundred to one. This is actually a useful method, not just a television act. The way to use counting for relaxation is to tell yourself mentally, "With every number down I am becoming more and more relaxed." I usually recommend people count from twenty to one. You can count down one number with each exhale. Let the body breathe easily and slowly. There is no rush—the whole point is relaxation. So take your time, nice and slow. By the time you reach the number one, you will find yourself much more relaxed.

Another method is to count rapidly from one hundred to one. Imagine you are riding an express elevator down to the deepest level of a subterranean learning center. Tell yourself before you begin that with every number down you will become more and more profoundly relaxed. Using words like "profoundly relaxed" opens up entirely new possibilities to the mind, and allows you to experience levels you may have literally never felt before. Can you imagine what it would be like to be profoundly relaxed, or profoundly happy?

Imagery

Imagery can be used for deep relaxation. One effective approach is to think of some relaxing, pleasant experience you have had. This might be sitting in front of a crackling fire. It could be soaking in a hot tub. Perhaps it is lying in bed in fresh flannel sheets, or sitting in the forest by a stream in the sunlight. Remember the one thing that is the perfect relaxation image for you. Using an actual experience is an effective way to access relaxation. Remembering a real experience brings back the feelings of that moment, including the body feelings. So a relaxing memory will automatically access the physical feeling of relaxation. If no relaxing memories come to mind, you can create a pleasant mental image. Any relaxing imagery will work. Imagine yourself in a warm pool, sitting in a mountain meadow, floating on a cloud, melting into warm sand, anything you like. Just pick something that makes you happy and comfortable.

DEEPENING

Beyond relaxation are a number of other important deepening strategies that we can use to take us further into the trance state. Although relaxation is very helpful in its own right, and a common ingredient in the hypnotic process, it is typically used as a transition into other deepening methods. This is because the relaxation process is more physical, more body-oriented. Focusing on relaxation can keep awareness on the physical body, which can be limiting. In hypnosis we want to leave body-awareness behind and drop into a deeper, more absorbed mind space. For this reason other deepening methods are generally employed in addition to relaxation.

Deepening Practices

In this section we will look at a variety of other methods for deepening. We can often go deeper through the doorway of the mind, as the mind is less constrained than the body by time and space. Try each one and see which you like the best.

Direct Suggestion

It always strikes me as interesting that the human mind responds to something as nebulous as "going deeper," and yet it does. The simple direct suggestion for deepening our self-hypnosis is "I am going deeper and deeper." As a result of that statement you will find yourself going into a more internally quiet place. You can also employ any equivalent phrase, such as "I am going deeper and deeper into trance," or "I am going into peace, comfort, heaviness, quiet." Hypnotists used to say "deeper into sleep," but I personally do not like to associate this state with sleep. Sleep and trance are very different from each other. Some people like the phrase "higher and higher." That is fine. It is a good idea to be consistent, however, in your phrasing and imagery. Since a lot of the imagery has to do with floating down, and the relaxation wording refers to heavy and relaxed, the idea of going deeper has a certain logic to it. As long as there is some consistency to your pattern, however, you can choose whichever wording feels right to you. Trust your feelings. Go with your own flow. Play.

Counting Down

You can count yourself deeper. The basic method is to tell yourself, "With each number down, I go deeper and deeper into trance." Then slowly count down, mentally feeling yourself going deeper with each number. In self-hypnosis you can count from twenty to one, or ten to one. Count one number down with each exhale, breathing slowly and deeply. This gives a natural rhythm to the counting. With each number remind yourself that you are going deeper. This method is similar to counting sheep to fall asleep. With practice the body and mind will become accustomed to going into an altered state as you count down. You can begin training your mind for this response by counting from fifty to one. Every few weeks reduce the count by ten until you reach ten to one. You can then use ten to one as your count. Your mind will become used to this deepening method and will be able to attain a deepening state of comfort easily. As this method is essentially the same as counting into relaxation, you can combine the wording to go deeper into relaxation and deeper into trance simultaneously.

A related deepening method is to find a noisy clock, one with a substantial "tick-tock" quality. Wind it up tight and put it near you when you do your self-hypnosis. Tell yourself that with each tick of the clock you will go deeper and deeper into trance. You can count back with every "tock" or just listen to it with the intention that the passing of each moment will take you deeper.

Visual Imagery

Imagery is a very useful tool in self-hypnosis. For deepening purposes you will want to use quieting and focusing imagery. These deepening images often possess a spatial-movement quality, such as a stairway, or a forest path. You can also use images of things floating, circling, or moving slowly and rhythmically, such as a feather floating down, a pearl sinking in warm water, or a wave washing over the beach. Another class of deepening imagery is to just select an image of a safe, comforting, pleasing place. Because this place is compelling for you, it will naturally draw the mind in. It can become your self-hypnosis inner power spot.

Deepening Images

The following list provides some examples of imagery patterns that my clients enjoy. Play with them to see which ones work well for you. You can also create your own. It is easy. One method is to simply remember one of the most comfortable, relaxing, healing, empowering places you have ever been. Use that image in your self-hypnosis to re-create that same incredible feeling within. You can also create a place. It does not have to be real. You can imagine the perfect place that makes you feel incredible. Make it safe and pleasing to the senses. Make it incredibly healing and empowering. It is all in your mind, so make it as perfect as possible. Be generous in giving yourself the most empowering, healing, amazing place you can come up with. You deserve it. Getting in the habit of building happiness inside will help create it outside, too. Be generous with your dreams.

Canyon Walls: You are walking down into a canyon. The air is fresh, filled with the scent of pine. The red walls feel smooth and warm. It is very quiet. Far below you the blue-green thread of the river flows gently. Hearing the sound of a bird, you look up to see an eagle circling over the canyon. It descends slowly, going deeper and deeper into the canyon with you.

51

Express Elevator: You are in an elevator at the top of a sky-scraper. You are watching the numbers as the elevator goes down to the first floor. It is a very fast express elevator. You feel yourself going down, going deeper. The elevator moves amazingly fast. It passes the first floor and continues descending. You finally reach the very deepest subterranean level where your private workspace is. You get out and enter a brilliant crystalline cavern far beneath the earth.

Forest Path: Walking down the beautiful forest path, you feel joyful. You can hear a stream flowing in the distance and birds singing in the trees above. The warm sunlight pours down gently upon you. You continue hiking farther into the forest. You are on your way to visit your friend, a wise old sage. You know that this is a very significant journey for you. On this journey you will receive important information and profound healing. You continue to go deeper and deeper into the forest.

Stairs: You are walking down a set of beautiful stairs. They lead into a garden (or into a warm pool, or liquid light). The stairs are very beautiful, warm red brick with green ivy on the wall. The old brass rail is smooth. You feel that you are going deeper and deeper into an amazing healing place. You feel your power growing.

Hypnotic Phenomena

Hypnotic phenomena are a specific set of perceptual and behavioral experiences that can occur spontaneously during trance, and that also can be intentionally evoked to deepen trance. These phenomena are natural to the human experience.

They include age regression, analgesia, catalepsy, hallucination, time distortion, and posthypnotic suggestion.

Although it might not be immediately obvious, we do commonly experience these phenomena throughout the course of a week. For example, do you ever think you hear the phone ringing while you are in the shower (and it is not ringing)? That is auditory hallucination. Have you ever lost track of time during a good movie? That is time distortion. Have you ever had memories of your own childhood when you heard a child laugh or cry? That is age regression. All of these normally occurring perceptual shifts are used in hypnosis. In that context they are known as hypnotic phenomena. They are useful in hypnosis as they help capture the attention and thus significantly enhance deepening. So let us take a quick look at creating or eliciting the hypnotic phenomena for the sake of deepening trance.

General Principles of Hypnotic Phenomena

There are two ways to deepen the trance with hypnotic phenomena. The first way is to give yourself the suggestion that you will go deeper into trance as the hypnotic phenomenon occurs. For example, "As my eyelids become locked together (hypnotic phenomenon of catalepsy), I go deeper and deeper into trance." This is basically pairing together the idea of deepening with the experience of the hypnotic phenomenon. The second way is to test the phenomenon. Using the eyelids example again, if you tried to open your locked eyelids, and you could not, you would go more deeply into trance. Deepening occurs in that case because the test (trying to open the eyes and being unable to do so) provides a confirmation to the mind that you are now in an altered state.

Now we are going to examine some specific phenomena. There are practices with each one for you to try. This will help you see which ones work best for you. All of them are fascinating and effective for deepening. When you use these hypnotic phenomena, remember to finish your session by telling yourself that the phenomena are released. Just give your mind the opposite instruction from the hypnotic phenomena instruction, such as, "My eyelids now open easily and feel wonderful." Your eyelids would naturally release when you return to normal consciousness even if you do not undo the phenomenon, but it is generally a good practice. Have fun.

Specific Phenomena

Age Regression

In age regression you are reexperiencing something from the past. That past could be yesterday or forty years ago. The depth of the regression will determine the vividness of the memory experience. It is common for people to remember things they have not thought about for years. They reexperience the original moment as if they were there. It can be very amazing. (Probably the most amazing thing about it is that so much life movie data is stored away in us somewhere.) Regression can be useful for remembering positive things about our life, for reworking stuck areas and limiting experiences, and for creating a healthier past image. I was recently working with a fifty-three-year-old client. She had an extremely vivid experience of being back in her childhood home in Holland, seeing people and places long forgotten.

Practice: A useful regression method is one I call Equivalent Affect Regression. In this method you go back into a past experience that elicits a specific feeling that would be useful right now. For example, whenever I need to feel persistence and increased energy I remember a time when I was running down the narrow mountain paths at Castle Crag Park. It was a hot summer day and I felt absolutely incredible—a total peak experience. I go back to a specific memory of that run (that is a regression) and I instantly feel more power in my body, more vitality, passion, and a willingness to keep going. Invoking the memory invokes the feeling. This is a very useful strategy for quick treatments, such as before an athletic performance, or an exam, or a cold call. Just remember a past episode of courage, strength, compassion—any success memory that elicits the appropriate feeling you need right now. Once remembered, you will be in that state. As a general strategy, before you do anything important, access a powerful success memory, a memory of something you are very good at, something fun. This will take you into a success state. I often think of a specific moment of downhill skiing in Colorado, and that rush is all I need.

Anesthesia and Analgesia

Anesthesia is the removal of sensation. Novocain at the dentist's office is an anesthetic. Analgesia is the removal of pain. An aspirin is an analgesic. With an analgesic you can feel other sensations, such as warmth and vibration, but you do not feel pain. Hypnosis can create both types of sensory modifications. These experiences do occur naturally. An example is when your arm falls asleep after you have been lying on it, or when a runner goes far enough to activate the runner's high in which the body does not feel as much discomfort or pain. These are all examples of this normal body and mind capacity. Although this method is more useful as a hypnotic treatment for pain, it can be used for deepening, too. We will come back to it when we talk about pain control in the applications section in Chapter 9.

Practice: Tell yourself as you are deepening that your hands are becoming so heavy that they are just dissolving. You can no longer feel them. Keep repeating to yourself that they are becoming more relaxed and heavy, that they are just dissolving. You are unable to feel them. They have no sensation. They are heavy and numb. They are gone.

Catalepsy

Catalepsy is paralysis. It is a very powerful form of induction and deepening. The inability to open the eyelids when they are hypnotically locked together is an example of this (refer to the inductions in *Chapter 4*). When the eyes are stuck shut, and we try unsuccessfully to open them, we get confirming evidence that we are in an altered state, so the trance goes deeper. Catalepsy can be applied to any body part or to the entire body.

Practice: If you are doing hypnosis sitting down, it can be interesting to make the lower body immobile. To do this, tell yourself that your feet are becoming fixed to the floor. Feel them becoming heavy and immovable. As they do this, tell yourself that you are going deeper into trance. Try to lift your feet to test it. Another simple method, if you are lying down, is to tell yourself that your entire body is getting more and more rigid, immovable. Feel yourself deepening as your body becomes more rigid.

Hallucination

A hallucination is a sensory misperception. Hallucinations can occur in any sensory channel—smell, taste, sight, hearing, or touch. An example of an auditory hallucination would be to hear the sound of an imaginary ocean gently rolling in and relaxing you. A taste hallucination would be to experience an imaginary taste in your mouth, like the taste of honey, or a pear. I was working with a client once who experienced an extremely vivid smell of jasmine while in trance. She thought I had sprayed something in the air. It was late winter and there was no jasmine or jasmine scent present. Jasmine, interestingly, was her beloved grandmother's favorite flower.

Practice: Tell yourself as you are deepening that you are having a vivid experience of some specific taste, smell, sound, touch or image. I often use an imaginary voice to guide me deeper inside, or I imagine the smell of some pleasant flower, or a warm breeze on my face. Choose a sense channel that is strong for you. Then pick some sensory experience that you enjoy and imagine that experience, telling your mind that you are going deeper as you access it.

Time Distortion

Time distortion uses the subjective experience of the passage of time to alter reality. If we can lose track of time, we have one less reference to the linear world of the conscious mind. In the dream world time has little meaning. Memories of things long past are as viable as the present moment. In hypnosis we use this natural capacity of the mind to play with both the direction and the pace of time to help us go more deeply into trance.

Practice: Tell yourself that you no longer know what day it is, what time it is, what month it is. You can tell yourself that you feel like you have been in trance for a long, long time. One of my personal favorites is to experience the eternal. It is always right here if we can find it and open to it. Just repeat to yourself that you are in an expansive, timeless place. This can make a relatively brief session feel much longer—infinitely long to be more precise.

Posthypnotic Suggestion

Posthypnotic suggestions are secondary suggestions that are used to help increase the effect of the primary hypnotic suggestions. They do this by providing cues or triggers to reactivate the primary suggestions during the day. We give ourselves these suggestions during the trance session. For example, you can use a hypnotically suggested trigger stimuli, such as seeing the clock on the wall in the exam room, to remind you to stay calm during the exam. In this case the Posthypnotic Suggestion given in trance would be, "When I see the clock on the wall during the exam, I will feel deeply relaxed and confident." There is a suggestion that after the session (posthypnosis) a clock will trigger the relaxation and confidence we are suggesting (primary suggestion). We will examine the process of posthypnotic suggestions in more detail in the next chapter.

CREATING A SAFE INNER SPACE

You will want to create for yourself a sense of safety if you plan on working very deeply. A sense of safety will enable you to let go and explore openly. You can use whatever method you know of for securing this sense, such as surrounding yourself with light, stating that you will be guided, or working with an ally. The latter can be a powerful method. If you work with an ally, such as an angel, then have that angel be with you, perhaps holding a golden strand attached to your ankle, during your session. That is a method I use for some of my deepest work. The important thing is to create a sense of comfort in doing the work so that you can go as far as you need to go. Knowing that you are safe will help you go further.

Also, when you do begin to go more deeply it is valuable to acknowledge your inner mind for assisting the process. You are involved in a relationship with a profound inner resource when you do this work. It is a partnership between you and your inner wisdom. It is important not to take that relationship for granted. When I come out, I thank my deep mind for helping me with my process. When my life begins to noticeably change as a result of that work, I congratulate my deep mind for our success.

SAMPLE RELAXATION AND DEEPENING METHODS

Relaxing the Whole Body

It feels good to relax the entire body. In this particular method you will learn how to do that. You will start at the toes and work up to the top of the head, relaxing each area of the body step by step. First get comfortable, lying down or sitting. Then take several deep, releasing breaths. Begin to bring your awareness to your toes, feet, and ankles. Take a deep breath and tell this area that it feels warm, heavy, and relaxed. Imagine that the joints and muscles are letting go. The joints are releasing and the muscles melting. Speak to those areas and take a few moments to really feel those feelings. Move up to the calves, knees, thighs, hip joints and tell them that they feel warm, heavy, and relaxed. Imagine that the joints are releasing and muscles melting. Speak to them and feel those feelings. Repeat this at the region of the pelvis and lower abdomen. Then the lower back. Then the chest and upper back. Then the fingers, hands, and wrists. Then the forearms, elbows, and shoulders. Then the head, neck, and face, focusing on the mouth, eyes, eye brows, forehead, ears, and scalp. Then relax the entire body. As you are moving through the body, tell each part that it feels warm, heavy, and relaxed. Imagine the joints releasing and stretching out comfortably, and the muscles just melting and sinking down. Feel the body feelings. When you have gone through the whole body (five to ten minutes), you can repeat the process or just lie there focusing on how deeply relaxed the entire body feels. This practice can be very helpful with insomnia. Often, by the time you get to your head, you will be asleep if you do this practice at night in bed.

Quick Relaxation

Smiling is a simple, powerful intervention. When you need a quick dose of positive energy and tension release, try smiling. If no one can see you, or if you do not care, make it very big. Enjoy the feeling. It might even make you laugh. Research shows that smiling actually releases endorphins in the body that help us to feel better. One of the extras I include in my smile practice is to imagine a loud applause from the audience (auditory hallucination). That creates even more positive energy, which helps to move the clouds away faster. A final touch is to take a deep breath, then smile, and then exhale with a sigh. Feel yourself releasing any pent-up tension. It is a very quick and effective way to change your state.

Deepening with Hypnotic Phenomena

Pleasant Past Projection

This technique is an example that uses hallucination and regression. Sit comfortably. Find a place where you can look forward at a plain surface, like a wall or the floor. Close the eyelids about halfway, allowing the gaze to relax. Ask your inner mind to show you a projected image of a pleasant past experience, something you experienced within the past few years. The image may appear as a still picture or as a movie. It may be clear or unfocused, color or black and white, complete or fragmented. Let it appear in whatever form it comes and just observe it. Tell yourself that this experience takes you deeper and deeper. Enjoy it.

Chapter Six:
Developing Powerful Suggestions

HYPNOTIC SUGGESTIONS

Induction, relaxation, and deepening prepare us for transformation. They access the creative inner mind and increase our receptivity to powerful new ideas. These methods help to make the mind a fertile soil. Once that soil is prepared, all we need to do is plant the seeds of our suggestions and watch them grow. In the previous chapters we learned how to prepare the mental field. The next thing we will learn is how to create effective suggestions to put into that field. High quality suggestions will make a dramatic difference in our outcomes.

In this chapter we will examine what hypnotic suggestion is. We will look at the construction of hypnotic suggestions, using positive languaging, working with imagery, direct and indirect suggestion, posthypnotic suggestion, and with concluding suggestions used to return from trance.

EFFORTLESS CHANGE

One of the unique things about hypnotic suggestion, something that can take time to truly appreciate, is that hypnotic suggestions produce change effortlessly. You give the hypnotic suggestion to the inner mind, and that mind then takes over. It begins working to find the necessary inspiration, energy, commitment, and solutions to our issue. As that inner process evolves, insights and new patterns begin to emerge. You find yourself changing, seeing things differently, behaving more powerfully. Your goal starts to move towards you.

Everyone has probably had the experience of studying or practicing some skill, such as playing the piano or doing math, and then putting it aside for a while. When you came back to it months later, you found that you improved somehow. Something integrated inside of you during that time. Even though it was not a conscious process, you learned new things and you grew. It all happened beneath the surface without conscious effort. That is how hypnotic suggestion works.

I remember a humorous personal experience that showed me the power of hypnotic suggestion. I was teaching a class on hypnotherapy. Two of my students were doing a hypnotic double induction on me. My request was to receive suggestions to get up earlier and to exercise more. They began their inductions, and in no time I was in a deep trance state. When they brought me back, I had no recollection of anything they had told me. They looked at each other mischievously and laughed. I did too. Well the next morning before the alarm went off, I jumped out of bed at 5:00 a.m. and decided it would be a good morning for a bike ride. I got on my bike and rode down to the beach. I proceeded to jump in and go for a swim (which is pretty crazy at 5:30 in the morning as the ocean is very cold where I live). That intensity lasted for a little less than a week before it began to even out somewhat (halleluja!). Since then I have been a firm believer in the power of the trance mind to manifest positive changes and new insights without our conscious knowledge of the process or our conscious effort to change. In hypnosis the process does not have to be conscious. The change just happens. It comes about as a consequence of appropriate suggestions given to that deep inner mind. Actually it is often preferable if the inner mind is allowed to do its work without conscious meddling.

AFFIRMATIONS COMPARED TO HYPNOTIC SUGGESTIONS

This notion of unconscious or inner process suggests an important distinction between hypnosis and affirmation. Certainly affirmation practices are very powerful. I use them often myself. However, they work more at the conscious level. We repeat the positive phrase in our conscious mind. The problem with that is that the conscious mind is not necessarily as open to new information. That mind is the pseudo-logical mind, which maintains the personal limiting beliefs about self via the inner critic, doubter, worrier, complainer, and other voices. It logically defends and maintains those old patterned beliefs. That mind is the internal bureaucrat. It serves to maintain the status quo, even if that status quo is totally dysfunctional.

The unconscious deep mind, however, is a flexible and creative place. It is a dissecting, examining, synthesizing, creating, learning mind. It functions like the child's mind, always building things up and breaking them down again in order to understand the universe. This mind can take new ideas and work with them. It is like our dream mind in which all things are possible, where even strange new things are believable. When we place our suggestions or ideas in at that deep level of trance mind, they meet with less resistance.

There they meet a creative ally that will work to find ways to help us reach our specified goal. That is the reason for using induction and deepening rather than just giving ourselves a conscious suggestion or affirmation. Conscious mind suggestions are certainly useful, but generally they have more inertia and bureaucracy to deal with, and consequently they are slower, less creative, and less productive.

CLEAR GOALS AND POWERFUL SUGGESTIONS

Because the deep mind is a powerfully manifesting state, it is important that our suggestions accurately reflect our goals. Clarity, to the extent we can reach it, is important. My experience in working with many people, and in my own life, is that the clearer you are regarding what you want, the more likely it is that you will get it. When you get clear, half of the work is already done.

I recall a time I wanted to buy a car. I spent three months looking for the right one. I went to an international auto show in San Francisco, read reviews, did all the research. It came down to three cars, then finally one, with a preferred color. That was it, I was clear. The next day I opened the local paper and saw my perfect car listed in larger than normal print. Being pragmatic, I did not get too excited. I went and looked. It *was* the perfect car at the perfect price. I purchased it and loved it for years. I had purchased another car before that with someone else's needs (goals) in mind. I never liked the car after the second day I owned it. What I had perceived as the other person's "needs" turned out to be a nonreality anyway. The lesson here is to get clear about what YOU want. Of course consider what is relevant to others, negotiate if others are involved in the decision, and then go for your highest happiness. You deserve to be happy. You deserve to have what you want. Be clear. Getting clear is a commitment to what you want. It says to the world; "I believe in myself. I am responsible and I take care of my life. My dreams and goals are important. I deserve to be happy."

ASK—AND YE SHALL RECEIVE

Be clear, and go for the highest good. You can ask for anything, but always keep in mind what really makes you happy. At the deepest level, many of the things we think we want are really just symbolic for something deeper. The big car is a need for respect. Having a partner may be a need to feel safe in the world. The thing desired is often not the real issue. It is the benefit we derive from that car, person, wardrobe. It can be very helpful to look at underlying needs to discover what benefits we are seeking. Often they are emotional benefits of safety, self-respect, love, happiness. Once you know that, you can work directly on that level, or you can work simultaneously on getting the car and building your sense of worthiness and respect. No matter what you ask for, it can be useful to include suggestions for these deeper foundation needs too—love, health, peace, happiness, courage, power, wisdom, generosity, abundance. They will help to provide more ultimately satisfying, healing, and empowering answers.

PRINCIPLES OF POWERFUL SUGGESTION

Here are some basic things you will want to consider to help you create the most effective hypnotic suggestions possible. We will examine three types of suggestions: verbal (*Chapter 6*) and visual and metaphoric (*Chapter 7*). Let us look at building powerful verbal suggestions first.

Verbal Suggestions

As the name implies, a verbal suggestion is a word or a phrase. It is like an affirmation except that it is given to the inner mind. To create the best verbal suggestions, develop them with the following ideas in mind.

Address the Issue

Make sure, to the extent you can know, that your suggestions are matched to the appropriate issue and goal. This means that you have a sense of what the real issue or problem is (as we discussed in *Chapter 3*). It is also important that your target goals are based on your deeper values and needs. If your goals do not match your values, those goals can encounter inner resistance.

It is great if we have a clear sense of the issue or challenge and the appropriate goal to work on. If you know that, you can make your suggestions very specific. If you are a skier, for example, you would give yourself specific suggestions regarding turns, carrying body weight, having a confident mental focus, and more. Sometimes, however, we do not know exactly what we need or want. In that case a more exploratory or open frame serves well. So if someone was trying to determine a career path, for example, and had no clear sense of what career they wanted to get into, then they could use more general suggestions. Rather than saying, "I will become a plumber," they would use suggestions for knowing how to find career information, meeting people who could advise them, making good decisions, and getting increasing career clarity. They could say, "My deep mind will help me to know what my perfect career is. I know it now. I love the work I am going to be doing. It is perfect for me."

Use Positive Wording

Generally we want to phrase our hypnotic suggestions positively. Which one sounds better to you: "You are really smart" or "You are not as dumb as I thought?" Similar meaning, very different feeling. The same rule applies when we talk to ourselves or give ourselves suggestions. Make them positive. Make a list of the things you want to change, improve, increase, or decrease. Remove any limiting terms and make positive statements. For example, instead of saying, "I no longer eat so much junk food," say, "I now eat energizing, life-giving foods." Instead of saying, "My cancer is growing more slowly," say, "My healing energy gets stronger every day. Healthy cells now dissolve any unhealthy energy in my body." Instead of saying, "People no longer reject me," say, "People love to be with me." Instead of, "I am not missing the ball," say, "My average is increasing steadily and will continue to rise during the season." Use the active voice. Be powerful and positive.

Create Variations

Variety is the spice of life. Variety keeps the mind engaged. Similarly, it can be helpful to have a number of variations with your suggestions. You will want to present the transformational suggestions to your mind from a broad range of perspectives. Variety gives the trance mind more information to work with. Additionally, having variety probably means that you have thought about your goal in more detail, which can only help. If you want to lose weight, for example, you can suggest that you eat healthy food, you take samller, energizing portions, you exercise every day, and that your body gets lighter and stronger. This provides a comprehensive and varied palette of suggestions.

Creating variation in your suggestions may require that you understand your issue more deeply. Information abounds on virtually every issue today. Do not be shy. Those resources exist to help you. Go to a bookstore in another town if you need to. You can even do your research at home on the Internet. There is so much information available for you. Knowledge can be very liberating. Often just knowing some facts can relieve fear and doubt. Get as much information as you can and use the more relevant ideas in your hypnotic suggestions.

Continuously Cycle—Relaxation, Deepening, Suggestion

During your session you will want to give yourself your hypnotic suggestion(s) repeatedly. Soon we will be putting all of the parts together—relaxation, deepening, and transformational suggestion. During trancework you just keep cycling through those three elements over and over again. The first two, relaxation and deepening, keep the trance mind open. The suggestion is what guides the specific direction of the internal change process. You will want all three while in the trance session. Relaxation and deepening prepare the soil.

Hypnotic suggestions are the seeds. These two groups are the yin and yang of hypnosis. They need each other to be complete. Get the soil ready and then put in enough seed to have a good harvest. Repeat the relaxation, deepening, and suggestion during your process. Keep it cycling.

Focus on Present/Future Outcomes

Generally we do self-hypnosis to move toward some desired goal. We can do it to explore the past, but even exploration of the past serves to clear the path to an improved future. Exploring the past for its own sake is probably not the best use of self-hypnosis. Self-hypnosis is about moving forward and finding solutions. To this end it is important to phrase suggestions so they focus on the present and the future. For example, regarding personal money management and planning, you might rephrase the suggestion "I am moving out of this debt (past/present)" to "Money is flowing into my life and my investments and savings are significant (present/future)." We want to put ourselves into a successful present/future picture. This helps to pull us forward toward the dream and the desired goal. Someone quitting drugs would want to imagine looking successful now and a year in the future and beyond, being clean, sober, healthy, and happy. It is important to phrase some of the suggestions as if they were true now. To always phrase them in a future sense keeps the outcome in the future. Do some suggestions of success now and some of greater success later.

Limit Session to One Goal

When we start doing transformational work, we sometimes get inspired and try to fix everything at once. That is like trying to balance too many plates at once. Ultimately each issue gets less attention with that approach. Too little attention is like too little medicine. You need to take enough to get your desired results. Half the recommended dose does not produce half the effect, it produces no effect. You need the right amount. So in each session concentrate on one topic or issue. You can do lots of quick sessions throughout the day, so the number of issues is potentially limitless. At any one sitting, however, focus on one major goal assignment.

Personalize Your Suggestions

Choosing your suggestions from an affirmation book is acceptable. It is much better, however, to create your own. When you create suggestions with your own words and ideas, they will hold more power for you. Use your name in the suggestions. Also use ideas that motivate you. If you value being a good parent, for example, and your issue is reducing procrastination, you can suggest, "I am becoming more focused and productive, creating extra time and energy to be with my family." If you are a religious person, you could include ideas from your beliefs. This practice is called binding, associating the desired outcome with something important or motivating. I use it all the time when I work with clients. It can be very helpful.

Use Posthypnotic Suggestions Too

Another important suggestion given during the session is the posthypnotic suggestion. A posthypnotic suggestion increases the power of the session by retriggering key behaviors and feelings during the week (post—after and hypnotic—the hypnosis session). The basic principle behind the posthypnotic suggestion is this: When a specific triggering stimulus occurs, a specific response will follow, in the form of a thought, feeling, or behavior. For example, if you want to quit smoking, and you are one of those people who lights up every time the phone rings, then the phone could be a good stimulus cue. The following posthypnotic suggestion would be appropriate to include in that session. "Every time I hear the phone ring, I will feel totally enthusiastic about quitting smoking." The ringing phone becomes a triggering stimulus, and feeling good about quitting is the response. Then during the week when the phone rings, you have a surge of enthusiasm about being tobacco-free, and this helps you carry on. Posthypnotic suggestions magnify the effect of the session by retriggering positive responses all week long.

Conclude with Positive Exit Suggestions

As you come back out of trance you will want to give yourself conclusion suggestions. You can say, "I am coming all the way back out, feeling completely refreshed, relaxed, and very, very peaceful." If it is near bedtime, then you can come out telling yourself, "I feel very relaxed and ready for a deep, wonderful sleep." Do these concluding suggestions just as you are coming back out.

Chapter Seven:
Imagery as Visual and Metaphoric Suggestion

USING HYPNOTIC IMAGERY

Imagery is a process of seeing with the mind's eye. We experience this frequently throughout the day. We daydream, we see images from last night's television program, images of our childhood are triggered when we hear a youngster's laughter. As we have seen in earlier chapters, imagery is an effective tool for inducing and deepening trance. Now we are going to examine an additional important use—imagery as a form of hypnotic suggestion.

Just as we can use words to convey suggestions to the deep mind, we can also use images to convey suggestions. An "image" can include sound, smell, taste, and touch, but the visual element is emphasized. Because we can image anything we want, fanciful or real, there are no limits to what can be mentally conceived. During self-hypnosis we can see ourselves doing incredible things, like flying to the sun on a winged horse, skiing a perfect slalom in world record time, depositing large checks in the bank, healing an illness. Because imagery transcends time boundaries, we can imagine the ideal future outcome as tangible now. That flexibility makes this a powerful tool for delivering hypnotic suggestions.

Imagery begins to create a pattern in the mind, a picture of possibilities. This image map lays a foundation for hope and positive expectancy. If we use imagery to increase our belief that something is possible, that belief begins to generate a positive self-fulfilling prophecy. So using visual and metaphoric suggestions together with verbal suggestions creates a very powerful transformational combination indeed.

HOW TO CREATE A VISUAL SUGGESTION

Visual suggestion takes the target outcome and turns it into an image. Instead of stating or describing our outcome in words, we use sensory images to build it. The same principles used with the verbal suggestions described in the previous chapter are used with visual suggestions—make the images present/future-oriented, positive, issue specific, and personalized. Also make the visual suggestions as sensory rich as possible, including the appropriate sensory elements (sight, sound, touch, taste, smell). For example, imagine you had a goal of winning a marathon. You would create a comprehensive sensory display of that goal to incorporate into your session. That could include seeing yourself crossing the finish line ahead of all of the other runners; hearing the announcer calling out your name as the winner; feeling the exhilaration as you cross the line, arms extended up into the air; smelling the air as you slow down and breath in deeply. You want to make your target outcomes vivid pictures or movies, as rich as life. The imagery should reflect the total success you want.

If the visual image is vague, that is fine. For whatever reason, it may not be a clear picture or a strong feeling. Start with whatever depth comes to mind. If you only get a piece of a picture, work with that piece. You can take that piece of image and amplify it. Make it bigger, brighter, louder. If you get no picture, then pretend. Say to yourself,

"If I could see an image, what would it look like?" This begins to build the image at some level of the mind, whether you can actually see it in your mind or not. It is still there affecting you. You can use this pretend strategy to create very elaborate representations, even if you have no skill at all with imaging. This is a way to augment imagery with words. Verbally describe the image and then elaborate it with more verbal descriptions.

Give the Image Feeling

Pairing strong feeling with your images makes them much more powerful. When two people see a picture of chocolate cake, one person feels delight (the chocolate lover) and the other feels disgust (the person allergic to chocolate). Same image, different feeling. It is the feeling that makes the imagery powerful. Images elicit feelings and those feelings move people to act. If the image does not have a feeling associated with it, we can predict it will not be very powerful, compelling, or motivating. If you see yourself winning the Olympic marathon but sense no joy or excitement, it is not a very powerful image. As you work with imagery, you will realize that just imaging something that you want does not always produce strongly associated "I want" feelings. This is probably even more true when it is an image that you find hard to believe or one that you have less personal experience with. Especially in those cases, it is necessary for the visualizer to bring the appropriate feeling into that picture. On certain days, that will take some doing as the emotion will not be right there. It will become evident over time, however, that the images created with strongly associated emotion will have more energy and consequently more impact. Bring your images to life with strong feelings. Allow yourself to believe. Hold the conviction in your heart that your vision is going to come true. Leave no room for doubt. Act as though it is guaranteed. Believe in your dream completely and get inspired.

Be Specific

Constructing a clear image will help you manifest your outcome. If you want to live in a bigger house, then create that specific house in your mind. See it, believe it. By imaging exactly what you want in self-hypnosis, you are planting a powerful dream. It will begin to be reflected in your thoughts, words, and actions, moving you towards your goals. The universe hears that song and begins to support you and your dream, molding that vibration into a new manifest reality. To be vague with your imaging can be a quiet statement of unworthiness. Allowing yourself to behold your dream is a statement to your unconscious mind, "I deserve to be happy, and I am ready to be happy." Clarity is power. Clarity precedes commitment. Let yourself be as clear as is possible with your vision. See what you want.

See the Future

A general self-hypnosis practice we can use in every session is to image our desired future life. In this practice we envision ourselves doing, having or being the desired end goal. That future image begins to draw us forward. It becomes a self-fulfilling prophecy. Seeing is believing. The clear future image helps us begin to believe that the goal is possible. This method also makes us think deeply about where we want to go. It is a very useful process.

A related technique is to create an outcome icon—a single snapshot image of what you want your outcome to be. That could be a picture of a new car, seeing yourself being healthy and happy, holding lots of money in your hands, being on the beach with a wonderful, loving partner. Once you have a clear outcome picture, you can reinforce that goal all day by giving yourself inward microflashes of that iconic image.

Practice Perfectly

When you use inner images in self-hypnosis, you will want to choose positive, productive images. If you are seeing yourself doing something, then see yourself doing it perfectly. Give yourself room to be successful in your own mind. Just that alone is a good exercise for many people. Let the image be a success image. See the ideal outcome. It is not practice that makes perfect, it is correct practice that makes perfect.

Play with Your Images

Externalizing your images can show you a lot about what is going on inside. In addition to using your images internally during your self-hypnosis practice, it can be very powerful to put your inner images or feelings on paper. You can draw them, paint them, create diagrams, or do any other visual thing you are moved to do. Express yourself. Put it out there and meditate on it. That will give you increased awareness. You can also use this method to catalyze the manifestation of your desired life by creating an image of the life you want. It can be a drawing, collage of magazine images, clip art. Put it together as a composite of your ideal life. Include goals for health, home, income, work, relation-ships, whatever you want. Then use that image as a reminder and a visual suggestion of where your life is going. In addition to writing down my goals, which I do religious-ly, I use a one-page picture of my future as an inspiration. This comprehensive pictograph reminds me of my desired total life outcome. One picture is worth a thousand words. This image manifests itself over time. It works.

Target Your Imagery

Use specific imagery to bring yourself into appropriately powerful and positive states of body and mind. For this method you can use recall of actual positive experiences. You will want to remember experiences that bring you into the appropriate target body and mind state. For example, if you want to get energized before giving a talk, you could remember a radical downhill ski run—get into that body and mind memory state, and then go and give your talk. That talk will be more empowered. When you recall the image of an actual memory, you immediately access the body and mind information related to the memory. You feel those same feelings again of relaxation, confidence, power, anything you need. This can be a very effective way to quickly create or change a state.

HOW TO CREATE A METAPHORIC SUGGESTION

Metaphoric suggestion is another way to work with imagery. The prefix *meta* means, among other things, change, as in metamorphosis. So a metaphor is a way to rep-resent something (often abstract) as something else (often more concrete) in order to understand it better. Joseph Campbell, the great scholar of world mythology, spoke at length about how the world's ancient myths are metaphors for ideas that are more transpersonal and universal. The mythic masks, totems, ceremonies, and deities are metaphoric expressions of concepts more intangible and difficult to comprehend. So our human mind creates these metaphoric representations, such as deity images, to help us understand and relate to the mystery of life more fully.

Similarly, in hypnosis we can use stories and images metaphorically to convey more complex or abstract suggestions to the inner mind. For example, you may be seeking a sense of security and protection in your life. You could use an image of a bear as a metaphor for a protective quality to guard over you. That bear could then be incorporated into hypnotic imagery, being at your side, warding off negative forces. The key is to come up with images that represent the essence of the solution quality you are looking for. If you need courage, bring in a lion; if you need fun, bring in an otter; if you need healing, bring in the sun. Let these forces be with you, talk to you, and guide you, or become them and feel their wisdom within.

Metaphoric suggestions are also helpful as tools for providing new perspectives and insight. As an example, say you wanted to do very well in a sporting event, like speed skating. You could become an arrow in your self-hypnosis session. You would then feel what it would be like to be streamlined, cutting through the air, moving with total concentration toward the bull's eye. That experience would provide new information about speed and focus. This information is different than just imaging yourself skating fast and winning the race. It is an experience of *being* an arrow. It provides a different perspective that offers new information. The ancient shamans learned from animals this way by becoming the animal. Through this process they came to understand deeply that animal and its powers. The metaphor can be a very powerful direct sensory suggestion.

A final metaphoric strategy is one I call the Metaphoric Reintegration Process. In this approach you turn the challenging issue or feeling into a metaphoric image and then antidote it with a counter image. For example: take a pain sensation in the body and ask the inner mind to give it a color, shape, temperature, and sound. Then ask the inner mind to present you with the appropriate antidote color, shape, temperature, and sound. Once you have these two metaphoric representations, first notice the pain sensations and bring in the pain qualities—color, shape, temperature, sound. Then change the pain quality to the antidote quality while focusing on the painful area. Using this simple method begins to give you more control over your inner experience.

CONCLUDING THOUGHT

By using visual images and metaphors as suggestion in your self-hypnotic practice, you gain access to a tremendously flexible and powerful tool. With time, the ability to create rich imagery will grow, and you will be amazed at what a useful resource it can be.

Applications

Chapter Eight:
Putting It All Together

In this chapter all of the pieces come together. You will learn a useful format for doing self-hypnosis. Whenever you want, you can embellish this approach with ideas from earlier chapters and tailor it more specifically to your own preferences. Experiment and find what works best for you. Initially it will be helpful to choose an approach, such as the one provided here, and use that for a while. That will allow the body and mind to become accustomed to one path, making the trance process easier. If you drive the same route every day, it becomes easier to remember the way and to get to your destination. Having a consistent and familiar method will help you to go into trance more effectively. You can of course modify your approach as many times as you like, but staying with a particular form for a while can be helpful in the beginning.

THE SELF-HYPNOSIS FLOW

The Goal

As described in Chapter 3, having as clear a sense as possible of your desired outcomes is paramount. A vague goal will generate less insight, less commitment, and less motivation. Water becomes a powerful force when it is focused and directed through a fire hose. Give direction to your dream. The clearer the better. You can of course use hypnosis to arrive at greater clarity if you do not know the right path yet. Finding the clearest goal can become your goal.

The Setting

As mentioned in Chapter 4, we ideally want to do our sessions in a setting that is conducive to relaxation—one that is comfortable, reasonably quiet, and free from disturbances. If the lights can be lowered and some music turned on, that is great. Reduce external input as much as possible, so there is less stimuli to pull the mind back out into the world.

Obstacles

It is always useful to ask yourself if you are really willing to remove the obstacles from your life to make something happen. If not, then there may be little value in working on it now. If a person is not quite ready for real change, hypnosis can be used as a preparatory process. If someone comes for hypnosis to quit smoking, for example, and I know they are not ready, we prepare for quitting at some future point, rather than trying now and not succeeding. It is good to be honest about our willingness to succeed now.

The Suggestion

Think of the suggestions you will want to use. Make them appropriate, sufficient, positive, and varied. You will need a clear set of suggestions before you can do effective hypnosis. Work on the languaging of your verbal suggestion and the imagery and metaphors for your visual suggestion. See Chapter 6 for more details.

Induction

Choose your induction method. In Chapter 4 we presented a variety of methods for you to experiment with. The

Locked Eyelids method is a good one to start with if you have not selected another one already. It is simple and very effective for most people. Whichever one you choose, remember that patience and persistence pay off.

Relaxation and Deepening

Get comfortable. You can do self-hypnosis anywhere, but ideally, find a comfortable chair or couch to lie on. Make sure you stay warm enough, too. Use a blanket if you need it. You will remember from Chapter 5 that the magic words for relaxation are "Warm, Heavy, and Relaxed". Tell yourself over and over, "I feel warm, heavy, and relaxed." That formula is simple and effective.

For deepening you can use imagery, counting, direct suggestion, and hypnotic phenomena. One effective method is to recall an image of a pleasant place to begin your deepening. See yourself in that place looking very happy, healthy, and relaxed. Then count down from twenty to one. Tell yourself, "With each number down I am going deeper and deeper into trance." See Chapter 5 for details.

Suggestions

Give yourself your suggestions—verbal, visual, and metaphoric. Alternate your suggestions with relaxation and more deepening. Continue to weave the relaxation wording and images and other deepening methods to stay in the trance state while giving yourself your suggestions. See your outcome. Feel it. Tell yourself that you will achieve your goal. Believe it.

Conclusion

Time to come back. Tell yourself, "I am returning now, feeling refreshed, relaxed, and ready for the day. My eyes will feel just perfect, very bright and clear, when I come back. My arms and legs will feel very relaxed and easy to move again. I feel great. I am coming back to the best day of my life." Come back slowly, noticing your breathing and your relaxation. Thank your deep mind for the help that it provided. Give yourself the posthypnotic suggestion as you return that each session will be even more effective and that during the day the positive effects of this session will become more and more evident. You can say before coming out, "Every time I hear [a bird, stop at a red light, answer the phone, etc.] I will _____. " This posthypnotic trigger will help you to reactivate the desired thought or behavior.

GENERAL PROCESS SUMMARY

- **Induction Method**
- **Relaxation**
- **Deepening**
- **Suggestion** [Cycle—for as long as you want, cycle through your relaxation and deepening methods and your suggestions over and over to help you stay in a deep trance state while receiving your suggestions.]
- **Conclusion**

SAMPLE SCRIPT

The following is a sample script you can use for your own process. In the beginning you may want to read it to yourself for your self-hypnosis practice. As quickly as possible you will want to put the script down and paraphrase the concepts in your mind. You can modify this script with other elements that feel appropriate to you based on the ideas in the previous chapters. In addition, the next chapter has many ideas for working with very specific issues. You may want to look at those now and incorporate any ideas related to your target issue or goal into the script. Once you have all of your elements, you can make a tape for yourself if you want. It is easy to do and it can be a useful way of working on your goal. You can write a short script, fine tune the message, and record it. That whole process will probably take an hour or two. You will then have a very tailored product for your transformational process.

The Flow

Prepare the Setting

Before you begin, if possible, have a comfortable, quiet environment. Put on some peaceful music. Loosen up any tight clothes, take off glasses and shoes, get comfortable. If you have to be done in a certain time, or if you are concerned that you may fall asleep, you could set a quiet alarm for the designated time.

Begin to Change State

I will now take three deep breaths. Three slow, deep breaths. Each breath allows me to let go and to relax. Each breath allows me to let go of any tension and to feel my body begin to relax now. I am looking forward to going deep inside and finding whatever I need to make my life even more amazing. I know that everything I experience, every sound, thought or feeling, will help me to go even deeper inside. I will come back at the right moment with what I need to be happy, effective and successful.

Induction (Locked Eyelids)

As I continue to relax I notice that my eyelids are becoming heavier and heavier. They are wonderfully heavy, wanting to close. I know that when they close I will go even deeper inside. They are getting so heavy and so relaxed. They want to close and take me deep inside, into that wonderful [healing/creative/powerful] place. My entire body is getting heavier, more relaxed. Wonderful currents of warm energy are flowing through me. My eyelids are getting so heavy, taking me deeper and deeper inside. When they close, I will not be able to open them, they will be so heavy. They will not open until my session is done. They are getting so wonderfully heavy. (Repeat until eyes close.)

Relaxation and Deepening

My arms and legs are warm, heavy and relaxed. I am floating in warm water, just floating. It feels so wonderful. (Repeat several times.) *I am walking down a very long stairway* (describe). *With each step I am going deeper and deeper into my inner mind. It is wonderful. Twenty. I am sinking down. Nineteen. Feeling more and more wonderfully relaxed. Eighteen. My body and mind are going deeper. Seventeen. It feels wonderful to go so deep. Sixteen. Everything is becoming so relaxed, so wonderful. Fifteen. The stairs are helping me to go deeper. Fourteen. I am going deeper. Thirteen. Deeper. Twelve…Five. Deeper. Four. Feeling wonderful, profoundly deep. Three. Very, very relaxed. Eyelids so heavy, unable to open now. Two. So deep. One. Floating down deeper like a stone sinking in warm water. It feels wonderful.*

Special Place

I am in a most amazing place now. It is incredibly comfortable here. It is (describe mentally the colors, temperature, sounds, any special aspects). *I am deeply relaxed.*

Suggestions

As I enjoy this deep comfort even more, I begin to hear my inner [mind/teacher/voice/wisdom/soul/self] *speak to me of my future, guiding me. I go deep inside and experience the words and images going directly into my being. I am* [_____ hypnotic suggestions]. *I see myself in a year looking and feeling* [_____ hypnotic suggestions]. *I feel* [_____ hypnotic suggestions].

Deepening/Relaxation/Suggestions

(Repeat this cycle until done.)

I continue to go deeper and deeper, letting these ideas mix into my inner mind. My inner [mind/teacher/voice/wisdom/soul/self] *is giving me the answers from a deep place of power. I feel so incredibly relaxed. My arms and legs are warm, heavy, and relaxed. I am* [_____ hypnotic suggestions]. *I see the powerful positive energies of life helping me* (imagery or metaphoric representation). *I see myself achieving this goal so clearly* (visual imagery of outcome—see and feel). *My life is wonderful. I feel incredible. My dreams will come to me in the most positive way. I feel warm, heavy, and incredibly relaxed.* [_____ hypnotic suggestions] *comes true. I am going deeper and deeper into that dream. I will* [_____ hypnotic suggestions]. *My body and mind are going deeper and deeper. I count down from ten to one, and with each number down I know my* [_____ hypnotic suggestions] *will come to me. Ten, I am feeling such* [energy/peace/success/financial abundance/healing]. *Nine* [_____ hypnotic suggestions]…*One. During the week when I notice* [_____ some trigger stimuli, such as stop sign, phone rings], *I will remember this feeling of success and I will know that my goal is being achieved now. I feel excellent.*

Conclusion

My dreams will come to me. I can see my goal totally, clearly. I will take a moment to let this experience integrate deeply into my being. I take a deep breath and let the image of success go deep inside. I see myself looking very accomplished, very happy. I know that whatever is perfect and best for me will come to pass. I notice my body now, my breathing. My eyelids feel normal, comfortable, and refreshed. I am coming back feeling refreshed, relaxed, and ready for life. Each session will be more and more effective. This is going to be the most amazing week of my life. I feel incredible and I anticipate positive success all week long. I come out now feeling great.

End

Now open your eyes slowly and have an amazing day.

Quick Method

Try the **One Minute Method** described in Chapter 2, page 17.

Chapter Nine:
Specific Applications

In this last chapter we are going to look at a number of ideas for working with specific issues. In the previous chapters we have been building a format for self-hypnotic work. Now that the format is complete, you can begin to plug in specific information on issues of personal interest. The following list of topics provides information on many issues of interest to people working with self-hypnosis. If your particular interest is not found here, select something similar and use the same concepts. You can also go through the entire list and find the ideas that feel the most appropriate to you and use those for your own work. Be creative.

- Addiction & Habit Control
- Anxiety, Phobia, Fear, Stress Management
- Creating More Energy
- Optimal Health and Healing
- Insomnia
- Enhanced Learning
- Pain Management
- Self-Confidence, Shyness, Self-Love
- Sports and Performance
- Weight Management

Each topic in this chapter is approached comprehensively from a systems perspective providing ideas regarding the personal, behavioral and environmental elements of the issue. The Person component includes feelings, thoughts and physiological reactions. The Environment is the world outside, which includes the biological, social, and physical environments. Behaviors are the things we do and say as a consequence of that interplay between our person and the environment.

In addition there will be three types of suggestions provided for each issue—verbal, visual, and metaphoric. Verbal suggestions will be phrases that can be employed during the trance session. Visual suggestions will be images of the desired outcome that you will image at various points during your self-hypnotic session. Metaphoric suggestions are representations of the issue seen in another way, providing the potential for new insight and understanding. The three types of suggestions, in combination with ideas on the person, behavior, and environment factors, provide a lot of useful material for building a very powerful self-hypnosis flow.

Addiction & Habit Control
(Drugs, alcohol, tobacco, food, other)

Person: Dealing effectively with addiction involves working with emotional obstacles and physical anxiety. The underlying emotional issues can be difficult to find, understand and impact. These emotional causes may be about fear, unworthiness, helplessness, concern about not surviving, a desire to die. You can ask the inner mind to help fix whatever it is. Emotionally you want to develop a sense of self-worth, positivity, and capability. You will also need to develop your ability to relax and let go of tension, especially during initial abstinence as there may be physical anxiety and uneasiness. Get the body balanced again and remember that you deserve to live. Be patient, love yourself, be proud of yourself for doing the work. Do not give up. You can do it.

Behavior: Pay attention to the addiction pattern—when, where, why, how much. When you begin self-monitoring your pattern in this way, you make it more conscious. This helps awaken the change process. One behavioral strategy is to do the behavior differently, to break up the automatic pattern. For example, you can wait for a set time before you do it, do the steps in a different order, do them very fast, whatever you can think of to break it up. This helps some people make changes. Drop the old way. Find new ways to make your life work.

Environment: You may need to change elements of the environment to succeed at becoming independent. If you associate with other addicts, their addiction will challenge your new path. Most likely you will need to make new friends. That can be challenging, but we are talking about your life. You will also need to regulate your environment to keep away from the thing you are addicted to. Keep it out of your space and avoid places where you can easily obtain it. Ask for help. Join a support group. There are lots of twelve step programs and other resources around that can be helpful.

Verbal Suggestion: *I know I will survive. I know I am safe. I love myself and seek out others who respect themselves and who respect me. I am capable and I am learning new ways to make my life work better and better. I deserve to live. I deal with any urges easily and effectively because I am strong. I enjoy my life free of _____. I am balanced and healthy, and I only do those things that bring me true happiness, strength, peace, and balance. I associate with people who are healthy and strong. I no longer go to places that are not life supportive. I love who I am.*

Visual Imagery: See yourself as addiction free. See yourself one year and five years out in the future being independent, healthy and very happy. See yourself dealing with urges very effectively now. Image a relaxed, happy, confident you.

Metaphoric: Find a specific image that triggers a feeling, a specific feeling, that helps you deal with this change. For example, if you need to feel strong, you could use an image of a brick wall or a superhero. If you need courage, you may use an image of a lion. You could imagine a wise person if you need to feel calmness or guidance.

Anxiety, Phobia, Fear, Stress Management

Person: Relaxation is very, very helpful. Get the body vibrating at a lower, quieter level. Practice some relaxation method before a stressful event, such as right before an exam starts, or right before a performance. You can make fear a small brother or sister. Take it by the hand and walk with it, but do not let it run and drag you—keep it by the hand and walk together if it is there. Talk to that small, frightened child and reassure him or her. Also focus on your goal and feel your passion. This makes obstacles smaller or invisible. Go with your passion. And, very key, remember to breathe deeply when you are anxious. Inhale through nostrils, exhale through pursed lips. This will change your inner chemistry and help you relax immediately. Acupuncture can also be helpful.

Behavior: Reduce behaviors that increase your anxiety, such as procrastination and being late, alienating people because of your social fear, any other behaviors that increase your anxiety. Manage time, say no, get clear on goals, be responsible. You will succeed. Laugh, smile, do fun things, learn to be more at ease, get out of your head, go for walks at the beach, be responsible, listen to quieting music, reduce use of drugs and alcohol and stimulants such as coffee, keep your life in order, make more positive friends. Learn to meditate.

Environment: Reduce elements in your environment that increase anxiety, such as angry people, stressful work, excess noise, clutter, and other strong stimuli. Create a peaceful space. If you are dealing with phobia, seek assistance, as phobias are quite responsive to hypnosis. Work with a trained professional.

Verbal Suggestion: I am calm and relaxed. My body is warm, heavy, and relaxed. I move toward my goals. My mind is peaceful. I know I will survive. My negative thoughts are disappearing. I allow myself to be happy. I feel more and more relaxed.

Visual Imagery: See yourself as being very calm and relaxed. Image being in a hot tub, in a cabin in the woods, hiking in the forest. When stress inducing images come to mind during the day, modify the image, make them small, grayish, insignificant. See them vanishing. You do have power over them, and with practice that power will grow. Take the reins, change them, create positive images for every negative one.

Metaphor: Be like a warrior or fighter. Experience that warrior's force interacting with all things with incredible energy. Use this as a metaphor of immense power. Or be like a child learning, playing, and having fun with this challenge.

Or be like a wise person who knows a great deal about dealing with difficult things.

Other Ideas: With phobia we often find a clear interrelationship between person (negative imagery, internal fear feelings, and physical discomfort), behavior (avoidance), and environment (fear-evoking stimuli). One of the easiest ways to work with this trinity is to disrupt it at one of those three points. A very effective method is to induce a deep state of relaxation (opposite of body discomfort) when you think about the anxiety-provoking item. Work on deep relaxation; then bring in nonthreatening mental images of the fear-evoking stimuli. Flip back and forth between deep relaxation and the image. This will begin to create a new pattern, disrupting the old pattern of stimuli, fear, and avoidance. Be patient with the fear and with yourself and it will dissolve.

Creating More Energy

Person: Develop a positive mental attitude. Positivity will do a lot to create more personal energy. Give yourself inspirational talks. Imagine that people are applauding you, like you are crossing the finish line, a winner. Energize yourself mentally. In the morning sing yourself an "I feel great" song to build your positive energy for the day. Remember that you are a learner. You are learning what you need to know to be happy. Remind yourself over and over that you will succeed, that you can do it. Self-love is also very energizing.

Behavior: Eat foods that make you feel light, happy, clear-minded, and able to work. Avoid excess amounts of food. Also reduce alcohol consumption as it is a mild depressant.

Exercise will increase general well-being and energy. Keep your life balanced. Discipline yourself, in a positive way. Place your goals out where you can see them, to remind you of what you want in life. Track them and reward yourself for success. The clearer and more committed and more enthusiastic you are about your dream, the more energy you will run. Read about passionate people like Thomas Edison or John Muir. Passion is totally energizing, and your dream is a strong connection to passion. Live a life of no regrets. Go for it!

Environment: Get the junk food out of your house. Make it easy to exercise, buy a jump rope, move closer to the park, whatever is necessary. Keep images around the house that display active, energetic people, such as illustrations from sports or outdoor magazines.

Verbal Suggestion: I am powerful, alive, and dynamic. The energy flows through me. I feel great. I feel incredible. I love my life. I am powerful, productive, organized, energetic, and totally effective. I really love my life.

Visual Imagery: See yourself looking completely excited about life. You look extremely happy and fired up. Perhaps you are jumping up and down with your arms up in the air shouting, "Yes". See yourself energized and feel the power.

Metaphor: Become an animal that represents full energy for you. You could become a galloping wild horse or a tiger when doing a workout. Become something powerful and feel that power within you.

Financial Security & Prosperity

Person: Money is a mental symbol, a metaphor. What is it symbolic of for you—freedom, safety, abundance? Remember to go for your deepest values. If freedom is your core value and you gain a lot of money but not freedom, where are you? Always go for the deepest level of personal meaning. Money is a practical resource. Acquire it and use it wisely. It is important that you now embrace strongly the belief that it is very easy for you to make money.

Behavior: Set your financial goals for a year, five years, lifetime. How much do you want to be worth five years from now, twenty years? Get some reading materials on money management and investing. Remember, it is easier to be wealthy by living simply than by trying to make enough to live extravagantly. Be a pragmatic consumer. Do not be as easily manipulated by consumer consciousness as others. Spend wisely. Earn, save, invest. Ask your unconscious mind for help and ideas.

Environment: Find someone that you know or that you see on the news who represents financial success for you. Emulate that person, become them, think like them (just pretend you know how they think; it works).

Verbal Suggestion: I am abundant. Money flows into my life. I am grateful for what I have. My success will benefit the entire world. The universe supports my success. I deserve to be abundant in every way. My success will benefit the whole world. The path to financial success invites me and supports me.

Visual Imagery: Imagine yourself on a television program being interviewed as a very successful business person (or related success imagery). See an image of yourself in the desired outcome state. See yourself having the friends, house, car you will have. See it clearly.

Metaphor: You are the ocean. There are many streams and rivers that run down into the ocean. The ocean gathers and manages those resources well. It is also continually moving that water out of itself to benefit the land masses and life forms, as the ocean knows the water will return in an enriched form with soil and nutrients. It is a powerful win-win model that works very effectively. Be like an arrow moving to the target. You are flying fast and direct. There is nothing that can stop you until you reach your goal.

Optimal Health and Healing

Person: A positive attitude and a positive belief are very important. Hold strongly in your mind that you will be healthy and whole. Allow the mind to be working constantly on bringing more balance to the body. Every thought, negative or positive, produces some effect. Seek to increase the number of positive thoughts moving through you and reduce the number of negative thoughts.

Behavior: Do things that make you happy, bring you energy, help you to be optimistic, heal you. Eat right—food is the first medicine in ancient systems. Do what you need to get well. Be positive and proactive.

Environment: Associate with positive people. Stay in healing energy places. Bring healing energy into your environment, such as plants, positive pictures and books, light, and fresh air.

Verbal Suggestion: I am getting stronger and healthier. Healing energy is flowing into my body from a very powerful place in the universe. I feel strong and whole. The universal life force is moving through me.

Visual Imagery: See yourself as energetic, whole, and happy. Send healing energy (*pick a powerful healing color*) to any part of your body and mind that needs healing. Send healing sounds, words, or phrases to those areas, make them up, let them come from your deep mind. Let your deep mind guide you to take right action. Feel healing energy flowing through you, like an energy stream. Imagine there is a powerful being, like a healing angel, working on you. Receive the healing.

Metaphor: When you toss a piece of dirt into a pond, it sinks, disappears, and the surface soon becomes calm again. Illness is that piece of dirt sinking and disappearing. Your entire energy field is becoming balanced and harmonious again.

Insomnia

Person: Learn to relax. Do a lot of relaxation practice—warm, heavy, and relaxed. When in bed, focus on your body instead of on your thoughts and feelings. When the mind starts rolling away on some idea, bring it back into the body, focusing on warm, heavy, and relaxed body feelings. Relax the body from the toes to the ears. Stay positive and happy. Simplify your life if you need to. They say an honest person sleeps well. Having alignment of body, mind, and spirit creates ease and sleep.

Behavior: Try the counting method with the phrases warm, heavy, and relaxed. Count from one hundred to one telling yourself you feel more comfortable with each number down. Before bed do not exercise, study, or do other activities that stimulate the mind or body or emotions. Do not work too late at night. Avoid stimulants at night and avoid spicy or stimulating food. Warm milk before bed can be relaxing. People who get more sleep than they need will not fall asleep quickly at night. Get as much as you need, not more.

Environment: Create a peaceful sleeping environment with a comfortable bed and windows that can be easily darkened to prevent street light from disturbing you.

Verbal Suggestion: *I sleep deeply and soundly. I focus on my body when I go to sleep, noticing the feelings of heaviness and relaxation. My body is comfortable and heavy, my mind is quiet. I sleep deeply, feeling refreshed and relaxed when I awaken.*

Visual Imagery: See yourself being very heavy like a rock, sinking down into the bed. See yourself sleeping deeply and waking in the morning feeling refreshed, relaxed, and peaceful.

Metaphor: You are a heavy rock sinking down in the warm, soft sand.

Enhanced Learning

Person: A relaxed body and mind state is more conducive to rapid learning. Clear the mind of obstructive thoughts. Hold a positive attitude about learning. Love to learn new things.

Behavior: Have a time and place for study and practice, and focus on learning during that time. Discipline will pay off. Take time for relaxation and play too. Your mind will be clearer and your energy more focused if you have balance in your life. In Chinese medicine we see excess work as one of the causes of illness. There is nothing redeeming or altruistic about all work and no play. In ancient medicine that is considered unwise. It is your life, and this is the only one you have (for now anyway), so have fun, but not too much. Work gives meaning to life. So work hard and relax, stay in balance. Be patient and persistent. Things build one step at a time. Do a quick relaxation exercise right before you take exams. When you are in the exam room, do a one minute body and mind relax/focus. There are many brain foods on the market now, like gingko biloba and gotu kola. Also a good vitamin supplement with B complex can help. Eat healthy food and get your exercise. Be consistent in your studies. Long-term memory is best with regular study and regular review. If you cannot study over time, the next best thing is to cram. Cramming right before an exam is always a good idea anyway, if it is not too stressful, as the content will be refreshed in your memory.

Environment: Have a suitable study environment. If the one you have is not suitable, find another one, or get ear plugs, or do whatever else you need to do to make it work for you. You are unique. Honor your unique needs. Associate with other focused, success-oriented individuals.

Verbal Suggestion: I learn very, very quickly. The information flows into my body and mind and gets completely absorbed. I will be able to easily recall and use this information when I need it. It is coming in perfectly. I am studying and practicing. I enjoy my study and practice time and look forward to it. I feel relaxed and clear-minded when I study. I am having fun. This is one of the best times of my life.

Visual Imagery: See yourself studying, very focused, looking intense and confident. See yourself taking the exam, doing the performance, and everything is smooth sailing. You look and feel great.

Metaphor: You are a great library full of all of the information you need. More knowledge keeps coming in. You are a holder of knowledge and wisdom. Guardians move through the library, keeping things in order, putting everything in the right place. They know exactly where to find what is needed whenever anyone asks for it. The guardians help you to find things inside and they guide you in your search for new knowledge outside.

Pain Management

Person: Chronic pain can create additional emotional issues—anger, frustration, and depression. These will have to be addressed. Then of course there is the actual pain sensation. Hypnotic analgesia can help with this (see *Chapter 5*). You will also want to work with relaxation. When the body has chronic pain, it will often produce muscular tightening in the painful area in an effort to limit movement and associated discomfort. That tightening becomes a secondary source of pain and it reduces flexibility, causing other problems. Stay relaxed and positive.

Behavior: Pain can produce secondary gain behaviors. This means that people's pain can be reinforcing because it gets them extra attention and access to drugs that can create dependence. Secondary gains such as drugs and attention will reinforce the pain and make it harder to remove it. These secondary issues will need to be examined and dealt with if relevant.

Environment: Utilize the resources in your environment that may help you—physical therapy, acupuncture and herbs, massage, whatever else may be helpful. Beware of practitioners who want you to get frequent x-rays, and come back over and over. That often benefits them more than you. Be a conscious consumer. Also, associate with positive, fun people.

Verbal Suggestion: For pain: I am calm and relaxed. I feel the healing energy flowing through my body and through my pain. I love my body and work with it creatively and positively. My body feels great. Pain dissolves and my body feels wonderful. For secondary gain: I enjoy being drug free. I love myself and feel loved by the universe. I help myself. I take care of my needs and I let others help me as needed. I am very independent and capable.

Visual Imagery: See yourself looking healthy, taking proactive steps to healing, being positive and strong. See yourself as happy and energetic.

Metaphor: Become a tree. They are strong and flexible. Work with Metaphoric Antidotes. If the pain is cold, send it warm energy. If it is warm, send it cool energy. Ask your mind, "If the pain had a color, what color would it be?"

Then ask your inner mind what the healing, opposite color would be. Send the healing color to that area over and over again. Speak to the pain and find out what it needs. When it answers through the inner mind, seek to give it the positive, healing things it needs.

Other Ideas: For specific pain, like headaches, or menstrual cramps, or dental pain, send healing energy to those areas. Relax, send cool or warm (depending on your need/preference) and a wonderful healing color to the area. Create hypnotic analgesia in your hand (hand gets more and more numb, *Chapter 5*) and then place the hand on the area to transfer the analgesia to the pain directly. For dental work or some other type of surgery, you can suggest reduced blood flow, rapid healing, healing energy flowing in the area, minimal pain, and good feelings. Finally, pain can be a signal of other things, such as more serious underlying issues or unresolved emotional concerns. If the pain persists, see a medical professional to get an assessment. If the pain is a reflection of emotional issues, you may need to deal with the issue at the emotional level for the problem to really heal.

Self-Confidence, Shyness, Self-Love

Person: Learn to relax deeply. Remove critical self-talk. Fill your mind with positive beliefs about yourself. You deserve to be happy. Remember that you are a learner and you are learning new ways to be in the world.

Behavior: Take good care of yourself. Treat yourself with respect. Praise yourself for having the courage to heal your past. Learn to forgive and move on. Deal with denial and anger and hurt. Begin to focus on your gifts, your goals, your dreams. Take responsibility and action, and make your life wonderful. There is no one else in the world like you, no one.

Environment: Associate with people who respect you and who encourage your growth and self-love.

Verbal Suggestion: I love myself. I am a wonderful person. I am growing and learning every day. I learn new ways of being in the world. Life is great. Life is awesome. I feel totally confident, powerful, loved, and lovable. I want to share my gifts with the world. I love myself for who I am.

Visual Imagery: See yourself as a confident, strong, and generous person. Imagine a guardian angel who comes and tells you the positive things you need to hear about yourself.

Metaphor: You are a precious child. You are loved in the way strong and kind parents would love and encourage the success of their child.

Sports and Performance

Person: Use a lot of positive self-talk and imagery. Bring in powerful positive attitudes and beliefs regarding expectations for your success. Always rehearse in your mind. Practice doing the entire thing perfectly. Rehearse perfectly in your inner mind and get ideas about how to be even better. Always go for peak sports performance in your mind.

Behavior: Practice consciously with the intention of noticing your patterns, removing what is inefficient or ineffective, and increasing what works better.

Environment: Associate with people who are as good, or better, at the behavior as you. Learn from them. Find someone who is the best at what you want to do. Watch videos of them, follow their game, become them, emulate their swing, serve, steps. Try to find out how they train, what they eat, how they practice, what their mental game is like. Become that person and then integrate the essence of what makes them effective, tossing out the idiosyncratic elements of their style. Feel what they feel, see what they see, think what they think. Once it is in you, it is yours. Then it can be integrated and incorporated into your unique style.

Verbal Suggestion: I am excellent at _____. *My body and mind are totally focused when I do* _____. *Every ounce of my energy is channeled into an excellent performance. I love doing* _____.

Visual Imagery: See yourself doing an element of the game/match/performance excellently. See the crowd going wild in support of your performance. Feel the energy flowing through your body. You are intense and powerful.

Metaphor: You are a laser of focused power, a powerful animal, an awesomely tuned machine, a radiant being moved by a divine force.

Weight Management

Person: Create a positive attitude about your body and your ability to manage your weight.

Behavior: Eat the right food—lower in fat, higher in protein and complex carbohydrates. Avoid fad diets. Exercise is also a key ingredient. Make it something fun, part of a joyful way to be healthy. Think of total health, with weight management being just one part of a bigger picture. Make the process enjoyable.

Environment: Avoid eating at places that serve unhealthy foods. Keep your house free of inappropriate foods. Join a club or find other fun places to exercise.

Verbal Suggestion: *I love my body. I am healthy, energetic, and happy. I am at the ideal weight for my body. I feel great.*

Visual Imagery: See yourself as fit, healthy, and energetic. You are doing active exercise and having fun. You are eating healthy food and loving the energy it gives you.

Metaphor: You are powerful and physically toned like a jaguar.

Afterword

I hope your life affords you the chance to work with these new skills and to develop confidence with them. Hypnosis is a special gift. It is a key that opens up a secret world. It allows us to enter that deep space within our beings where we may explore the vast potentials of this experience called life. For those who find that key, the adventures are great. So the best of luck to you on your journeys. Remember to keep the light on in your heart, as it will always help you find your way back home. And wherever you go, may your learnings bring you to deeper peace.

Glossary

Deep Mind: The hypnotic mind, often referred to as the unconscious mind. The terms deep mind, inner mind, and unconscious mind are used interchangeably in this book.

Deepening: The process of going further into a subjective trance state, often involving decreased awareness of external stimuli and increased responsiveness to hypnotic suggestion.

Hypnosis: A state of altered consciousness in which the creative, learning, deep mind is accessed and available for transformative work.

Hypnotic Phenomena: A number of perceptual experiences, such as hallucination, time distortion, amnesia, that occur naturally as a result of trance and can be used intentionally to induce trance.

Induction: The process of taking the mind into the preliminary state of trance.

Metaphoric Reintegration Process: A method for working more concretely with abstract issues or concepts by using symbolic representations of the solution.

Relaxation: A psychophysiological state of reduced muscular tension, reduced respiration and cardiac output, and more peaceful ideation.

Self-Hypnosis: The process of inducing an altered state of trance by oneself for transformational purposes.

Visual Imagery: An innate capacity of seeing images mentally that can be intentionally manipulated for vicarious practice and learning, for problem solving, and for transformational insight.

Resources

Books

Bateson, G. *Steps to an Ecology of Mind*. New York: Ballantine, 1972.

Cheek, D. & LeCron, L. *Clinical Hypnotherapy*. New York: Grune & Stratton, 1968.

Erickson, M. & Rossi, E. *Experiencing Hypnosis*. New York: Irvington, 1981.

Hadley, J. & Staudacher, C. *Hypnosis for Change*. San Francisco: New Harbinger Publications, 1985.

Haley, J. *Uncommon Therapy: The Psychiatric Techniques of Milton H. Erickson, M.D.* New York: Norton, 1973.

Hudson O'Hanlon, W. *Taproots: Underlying Principles of Erickson's Therapy and Hypnosis*. New York: Norton, 1987.

Kroger, W. *Clinical and Experimental Hypnosis*. Philadelphia: Lippincott, 1963.

Rosen, S. *My Voice Will Go With You: The Teaching Tales of Milton H. Erickson*. New York: Norton, 1982.

Watzlawick, P. (Ed.). *The Invented Reality*. New York: Norton, 1984.

Resources

Music

Aeoliah: *Angel Love*

Anugama: *Shamanic Dream*

Arvo Part: *Te Deum*

Brian Eno: *Ambient 1/Music for Airports*

Carlos Nakai: *Desert Dance*

David Parsons: *Himalaya*

Dean Everson: *Ocean Dreams*

Deuter: *Ecstacy*

Environment CD's: (the sounds of Nature; crickets are nice)

Georgia Kelly: *Seapeace*

Gothic Voices : *A Feather on the Breath of God* (Abbess Hildegard of Bingen)

Hilary Stagg: *Beyond the Horizon*

John Huling: *Lost Oceans*

Jon Vangelis: *Opera Sauvage*

Kitaro: *Kojiki*

Paul Horn: *Nomad*

Pierre de la Rue : *Officium Tenebranum* (Gregorian chant)

Raphael: *Music To Disappear In*

Robert Whitesides Woo: *From Heart to Crown*

Steve Roach: *Dreamtime Return*

Other Titles in the Same Series
by Book Faith India

For catalog & more information, write to:
PILGRIMS BOOK HOUSE
P. O. Box 3872, Thamel
Kathmandu, Nepal
Tel : 977-1-424942, 425919
Fax : 977-1-424943
E-mail : pilgrims@wlink.com.np
Website : www.pilgrimsbooks.com